100 | Fondant Animal Cake Toppers

100 | Fondant Animal Cake Toppers

Make a menagerie of cute creatures to sit on your cakes

Helen Penman
U.S. consultant: Dianne Gruenberg

FIREFLY BOOKS

A FIREFLY BOOK

Published by Firefly Books Ltd. 2012

Copyright © 2012 Quarto Inc.

First printing

Publisher Cataloging-in-Publication Data (U.S.)
Penman, Helen.
100 fondant animal cake toppers : make a menagerie of cute creatures to sit on your cakes / Helen Penman.
[256] p. : col. photos. ; cm.
Includes index.
Summary: Step-by-step instructions on how to create animal models out of fondant.
ISBN-13: 978-1-77085-087-3
1. Fondant. I. Title.
641.81 dc23   TX791.P466 2012

Library and Archives Canada Cataloguing in Publication
Penman, Helen
100 fondant animal cake toppers : make a menagerie of cute creatures to sit on your cakes / Helen Penman.
Includes index.
ISBN 978-1-77085-087-3
1. Cake decorating. 2. Fondant.
I. Title. II. Title: One hundred fondant animal cake toppers.
TX771.2.P465 2012   641.86'539   C2012-901189-4

Published in the United States by
Firefly Books (U.S.) Inc.
P.O. Box 1338, Ellicott Station
Buffalo, New York 14205

Published in Canada by
Firefly Books Ltd.
66 Leek Crescent
Richmond Hill, Ontario L4B 1H1

Color separation in Hong Kong by Modern Age Pte, Ltd
Printed in China by Midas Printing International, Ltd

Conceived, designed, and produced by
Quarto Publishing plc
The Old Brewery
6 Blundell Street
London N7 9BH

Project editor: Victoria Lyle
Art editor: Joanna Bettles
Designer: Emma Clayton
Photographer: Philip Wilkins
Copyeditor: Chloe Todd Fordham
Proofreader: Caroline West
Indexer: Helen Snaith
U.S. consultant: Dianne Gruenberg

Art director: Caroline Guest
Creative director: Moira Clinch
Publisher: Paul Carslake

contents

about this book

This book shows you how to make 100 different animal toppers suitable for all sorts of celebrations. The book is organized as follows:

Topper Selector
(pages 8–17)

Looking for inspiration? Browse the topper selector on pages 8–17, choose your favorite design, turn to the page listed, and follow the basic instructions to create your fondant model.

Materials and tools
These lists ensure you have all the right equipment at hand.

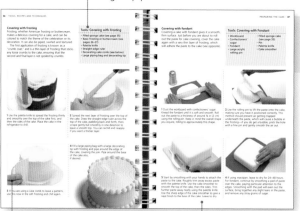

Tools, Recipes and Techniques
(pages 18–53)

Here you will learn how to bake and prepare the perfect cake to show off your topper, as well as information on tools and equipment and essential techniques such as piping, leveling and working with paste.

Step-by-step photographs
Full-color photography takes you step-by-step through the core techniques of cake baking and cake decorating.

Charts and tables
Measurements are given in imperial and metric. Choose one or the other; do not mix the two.

Topper Directory (pages 54–247)

The Topper Directory is a comprehensive library of topper designs that takes you step-by-step through the basic instructions to make cake toppers by building on the techniques learned in the previous chapter. Toppers are organized by theme as follows: domestic animals (pages 56–77), farmyard animals (pages 78–93), wildlife (pages 94–115), birds (pages 116–151), exotic animals (pages 152–183), underwater creatures (pages 184–207), reptiles (pages 208–216), critters (pages 217–233) and prehistoric animals (pages 234–247).

Warning
Wire is a choking hazard. If you use wire in your toppers, remember to tell the recipient that you have done so. Avoid using wire in toppers intended for small children.

Completed topper
Full-color photography illustrates the finished cake topper.

Skill level
Skill level (easy, intermediate, advanced) is indicated here. Start with an easy model and move up when you feel comfortable.

Materials and tools
Here you will find listed all the tools and fondant colors required to make the model.

"Start here" icon
The first step in the sequence is indicated by this orange icon. Start here and work clockwise.

Deconstructed model
Each model is uniquely presented in an "exploded" format, revealing individual components and how they fit together.

topper selector

Choose your favorite design, turn to the page listed, and
follow the basic instructions to create your fondant model.

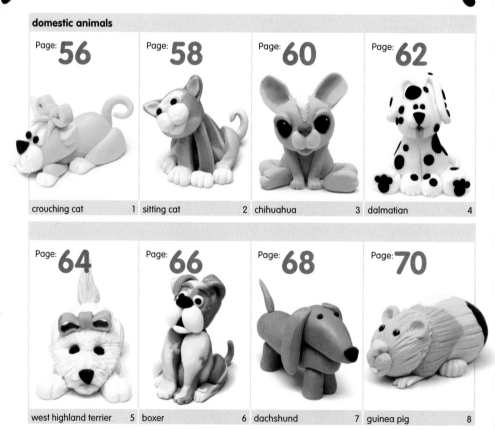

domestic animals

Page: **56**

crouching cat 1

Page: **58**

sitting cat 2

Page: **60**

chihuahua 3

Page: **62**

dalmatian 4

Page: **64**

west highland terrier 5

Page: **66**

boxer 6

Page: **68**

dachshund 7

Page: **70**

guinea pig 8

wildlife

Page: **96**

otter   21

Page: **98**

squirrel   22

Page: **100**

chipmunk   23

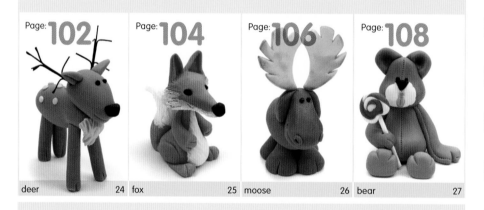

Page: **102**

deer   24

Page: **104**

fox   25

Page: **106**

moose   26

Page: **108**

bear   27

Page: **110**

porcupine   28

Page: **112**

raccoon   29

Page: **114**

beaver   30

birds

Page: **116**
owl   31

Page: **118**
blue tit   32

Page: **120**
chick   33

Page: **122**
eagle   34

Page: **124**
flamingo   35

Page: **126**
baby birds   36

Page: **128**
kingfisher   37

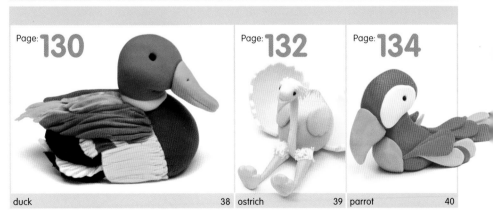

Page: **130**
duck   38

Page: **132**
ostrich   39

Page: **134**
parrot   40

birds

Page: **136** peacock 41

Page: **138** penguin 42

Page: **140** toucan 43

Page: **142** british robin 44

Page: **144** rubber duck 45

Page: **146** swan 46

Page: **148** puffin 47

exotic animals

Page: **150** woodpecker 48

Page: **152** bush baby 49

Page: **154** camel 50

exotic animals

underwater creatures

Page: **196** siamese fighting fish 71

Page: **198** sea anemone 72

Page: **198** shells 73

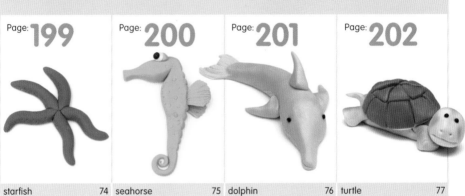

Page: **199** starfish 74

Page: **200** seahorse 75

Page: **201** dolphin 76

Page: **202** turtle 77

reptiles

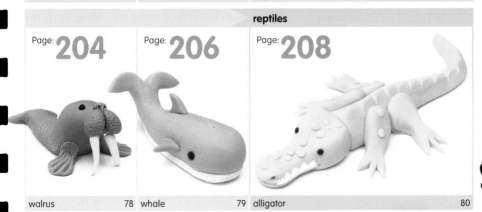

Page: **204** walrus 78

Page: **206** whale 79

Page: **208** alligator 80

reptiles

Page: **210**

chameleon 81

Page: **212**

bullfrog 82

Page: **214**

lizard 83

critters

Page: **216**

snake 84

Page: **217**

snail 85

Page: **218**

ant 86

Page: **220**

dragonfly 87

Page: **222**

bumblebee 88

Page: **224**

pink butterfly 89

Page: **226**

blue butterfly 90

tools, recipes and techniques

In these pages are all the essential techniques and materials you need to get started making your fondant models—plus recipes for cakes, frostings and fondants.

tools and equipment

The cake toppers within these pages are made using various sugarcraft tools; however, it is not necessary for you to buy them all. Instead, start with the beginner's tools (starred [✿] items below). Then, add to your supplies as you become more proficient and are ready to tackle more challenging toppers. Basic baking equipment is also required, and some kitchen tools are ideal for topper making, as well as for making the cake.

Workboard (1)
An acrylic surface is ideal for rolling and working on fondant pastes.

Pizza cutter (2)
A perfect tool to use when slicing and cutting long, smooth sections of paste. It is also useful when cutting freehand pieces that vary in width.

Small palette knife (3)
This tiny palette knife is sharp; it's useful for trimming paste, applying frosting to difficult-to-reach areas, and working on a small area.

X-acto knife (4)
The X-acto knife is a useful tool when you need to cut small pieces out neatly and accurately. It is also excellent for neatening paste in inaccessible areas.

Ribbon cutter (5)
A ribbon cutter can be altered to any width and will accurately cut out a ribbon of paste.

Cutters (6)
Various cutters are used throughout the book. Basic shape cutters, such as a set of round and square cutters, are invaluable, as are flower cutters. Think about building up a collection of your favorite cutters.

Decorating tip (7)
While this decorating tip is essential for piping, it can also be used to indent mouths and eye sockets.

Flower veining tool (8) ✿
Flower veining tools are the most important tools for model making. They come in all shapes and sizes, but what distinguishes them from other

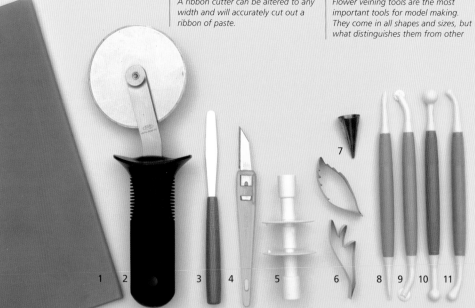

1   2   3   4   5   6   8 9   10   11

✿ Indicates beginner tools

modeling tools is that they are double-ended. One end is flat with a curved back for softening folds and smoothing out small, hard-to-reach places such as the inside of a small ear. The other end is pointed, which makes it ideal for veining flowers and making lines and creases.

Tracing tool (9)
A double-ended tool that has a tracing wheel at one end, while the other has a miniature wheel that indents the paste and leaves a stitch effect behind.

Ball tool (10)
The ball tool has two sizes of ball, ideal for smoothing, indentations, texturing and making nostrils.

Bone tool (11) ✿
This tool has a balled, angled end and is good for when you need to create holes or cavities, or enlarge areas. It is ideal for indenting eye sockets or ears, and for frilling or softening.

Paint brushes (12)
Used for edible glue, petal dust and paint made with powders. The fan paint brush is a fine brush good for detailed painting and applying a light dusting. Wash brushes with soapy water and dry with the bristles pointing upward.

Toothpicks (13)
Useful for adding color to paste, tweaking small, delicate areas of paste that your fingers cannot reach, and for smoothing and frilling edges of paste.

Lollipop sticks (14)
Lollipop sticks are useful to use as support as they are food-grade quality and give greater support than dry spaghetti.

Dry spaghetti (15)
Apart from being a delicious Italian pasta, spaghetti is excellent to offer support to paste, especially for more delicate areas such as paws and tails.

Cake smoother (16)
The cake smoother is a basic tool that is used to ensure paste has a smooth surface, and to remove fingermarks, ridges or creases in fondant.

Rolling pin (17)
An acrylic rolling pin is best as it is heavier and rolls paste smoothly. If you can't find an acrylic rolling pin, a household wooden one will do.

Foam pad (18) ✿
You can use pads of foam to hold paste pieces in place until dry or as a work surface when using the tools to mold the paste.

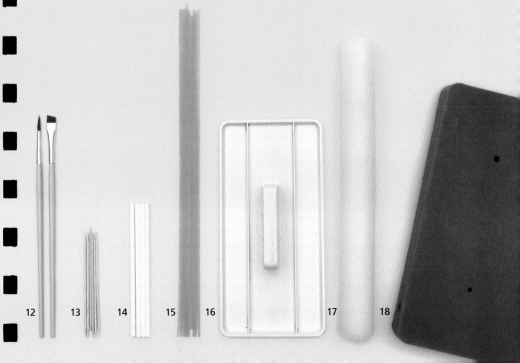

12   13   14   15   16   17   18

essential cake recipe

The cake topper must have a setting, so a cake is needed. Don't panic! Follow this recipe and instructions and you will have made the perfect cake for your topper. Various flavors of cake can be made with a little alteration to the basic recipe.

The first thing to decide is what size cake you need. This will depend on how many people are to eat it. The size guide (below) is based on pieces of cake that are 1 in (2.5 cm) square, which is sufficient if the cake is to be served after a full meal. If the cake is to be used as a generous dessert, the slice size will need to be larger.

Size Guide

Size of Cake	Round: Number of 1 in (2.5 cm) Square Pieces from a Round Cake	Square: Number of 1 in (2.5 cm) Square Pieces from a Square Cake
6 in (15 cm)	10	20
7 in (18 cm)	15	30
8 in (20.5 cm)	20	45
9 in (23 cm)	33	54
10 in (25.5 cm)	40	60
11 in (28 cm)	50	78
12 in (30.5 cm)	60	90

Classic Sponge Cake Recipe

The recipe chart (right) gives all the weights of ingredients required for each size of pan to produce a cake of good depth, around 3–3½ in (7.5–9 cm). You can also use this recipe to make cupcakes, dividing the mixture into baking cups. Always follow either imperial or metric measurements.

Flavors

Citrus
Add the juice and zest of one fruit for every 2 tsp (10 ml) of vanilla extract in the recipe.

Chocolate
Add 1 oz (28 g) for every 1 cup (250 ml) of flour. Add 1 tbsp (15 ml) milk for every 2 oz (56 g).

Natural Vanilla
Use the seeds from one vanilla pod for the smaller cakes, and two for the larger ones.

See also
Cake frosting, pages 26–27 > Pastes, icings, glues, pages 28–33 > Preparing the cake, pages 34–37

Round pan	6 in (15 cm)	7 in (18 cm)	8 in (20.5 cm)	9 in (23 cm)	10 in (25.5 cm)	11 in (28 cm)	12 in (30.5 cm)	13 in (33 cm)
Square pan	5 in (12.5 cm)	6 in (15 cm)	7 in (18 cm)	8 in (20.5 cm)	9 in (23 cm)	10 in (25.5 cm)	11 in (28 cm)	12 in (30.5 cm)
Unsalted butter	¾ cup (185 ml)	1 cup (250 ml)	1¾ cups (425 ml)	2¼ cups (560 ml)	3 cups (750 ml)	3⅓ cups (825 ml)	4⅛ cup (1.3 L)	4¾ cups (1.75 L)
Superfine granulated sugar	1⅓ cups (325 ml)	2 cups (500 ml)	3¼ cups (810 ml)	4 cups (1 L)	5¼ cups (1.3 L)	6 cups (1.5 L)	7¼ cups (1.8 L)	8⅓ cups (2.08 L)
Large eggs	3	4	7	8	10	11	13	14
Self-rising flour	2 cups (500 ml)	3 cups (750 ml)	5 cups (1.25 ml)	6 cups (1.5 L)	8¾ cups (2.2 L)	10 cups (2.5 L)	11.5 cups (3 L)	12¼ cups (3.06 L)
Milk	1 tbsp (15 ml)	1 tbsp (15 ml)	1 tbsp (15 ml)	2 tbsp (30 ml)	2 tbsp (30 ml)	3 tbsp (45 ml)	3 tbsp (45 ml)	4 tbsp (60 ml)
Vanilla extract	½ tsp (2.5 ml)	1 tsp (5 ml)	2½ tsp (7.5 ml)	3 tsp (15 ml)	4 tsp (20 ml)	4 tsp (20 ml)	5½ tsp (27.5 ml)	6 tsp (30 ml)
Baking time	½ hr	1 hr	1 hr 20 mins	1hr 40 mins	2 hrs	2 hrs 15 mins	2 hrs 30 mins	2 hrs 45 mins

Making the cake

Follow the instructions carefully when making your cake, paying particular attention to the addition of flour. Overbeating will make the cake heavy and dense.

1 Heat the oven to 350°F (180°C). Prepare the cake pan by greasing and lining the base and sides.

2 Beat softened butter and sugar together using an electric food mixer (or by hand if preferred) until fluffy and light in color.

3 Add one egg at a time and beat in thoroughly. If the mix looks as if it is splitting, add a teaspoon (5 ml) of flour. Add any flavorings now too (see Flavors, page 22).

4 Add the dry ingredients, sifting in a little at a time, and folding in gently by hand using a metal spoon or a rubber spatula. Spoon the mixture carefully into the prepared pan, smooth the top, then leave slightly inverted in the center. Place on the middle shelf in the oven. Check the cake once, 15 minutes before the end of the cooking time, but don't be tempted to keep on looking, since if you keep opening the door the cake will sink.

5 Test the cake using either a metal or a wooden skewer inserted into the deepest part. The skewer should come out clean.

6 Allow the cake to cool for 30 minutes before turning out onto a cooling rack. Follow the instructions on pages 34–35 to further prepare the cake.

Five Tips for Happy Baking

1 Heat the oven for 20 minutes before the cake goes in to ensure that the temperature will be at a constant from the start.

2 Place the cake in the center of the oven, not touching the sides.

3 Ensure that all equipment for making and baking is grease-free.

4 Always measure accurately, using only one set of measurements. Don't switch between imperial and metric.

5 Always grease and line cake pans correctly; it saves frustration later.

Troubleshooting

Cake sinks in the center
This is usually because the cake isn't cooked in the middle. Test the cake by inserting a skewer into the deepest part. If it comes out clean, it is cooked; if not, give it a little longer. Sometimes overbeating the cake at the batter stage can over-aerate it; this will cause it to sink during or shortly after baking. Always make sure you follow the recipe proportions correctly.

Domed/cracked top
This isn't really a problem since the cake can simply be leveled (see page 34). However, if when you fill the cake pan you make the center of the cake slightly lower than the edges, the cooked cake will have balanced out. The top has cracked because the outside of the cake has cooked more quickly than the center; the center then cooks and expands, cracking the top. A slightly cooler oven will allow the cake to cook at a more even rate.

Grainy appearance and dry cake
The cake mixture was not combined sufficiently and may also have contained insufficient liquid. Milk can always be added if the mixture looks too dry.

Cake is burned
The cake was left too long in the oven, or the oven is heating incorrectly. You may be able to resurrect the cake by cutting away the burned section, but take care that the flavor of the rest of the cake isn't affected.

Cake is too heavy/dense
This is usually due to too much flour, or overmixing the flour, so take care not to cross-weigh using two different units of measurement. The oven could also be too hot, so if this is a recurring problem, an oven thermometer might be a worthwhile buy.

cake frosting

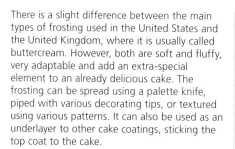

Cake frosting is any sweet, spreadable covering made of sugar, butter, water, egg whites or milk. It is often flavored, and sometimes cooked, and is used to fill, cover and sometimes decorate cakes.

There is a slight difference between the main types of frosting used in the United States and the United Kingdom, where it is usually called buttercream. However, both are soft and fluffy, very adaptable and add an extra-special element to an already delicious cake. The frosting can be spread using a palette knife, piped with various decorating tips, or textured using various patterns. It can also be used as an underlayer to other cake coatings, sticking the top coat to the cake.

Flavors and colors

Cake frosting can be flavored with almost any flavor you care to use. Frosting flavors tend to complement the cake flavor, with the frosting flavor being more intense; for example, chocolate cake with dark chocolate frosting. Alternatively, the frosting can add another flavor to enrich that of the cake, such as a chocolate cake with a Morello cherry frosting, or vanilla cake with lavender and elderflower frosting.

Frosting, like any other cake covering, can be colored using the same food colors used for modeling paste (see pages 38–39)—chocolate will naturally have its own color. Start with the basic frosting or buttercream recipes (shown opposite), then add the color.

If the thought of making the frosting is a little scary, or you are short of time, you can buy it ready-made at any supermarket or make the buttercream recipe instead, which is very quick and straightforward.

Quantities

The table below gives quantities of frosting ingredients required for different cake sizes to allow for two layers of filling within the cake. An additional quantity of the recipe is required for covering the outside of the cake.

Frosting Flavors

Vanilla
Add 2 tsp (10 ml) of vanilla extract or the seeds of one vanilla pod.

Citrus
Add the juice and zest of one piece of fruit.

Coffee
Add 2 tbsp (30 ml) of strong coffee.

Chocolate
Add ¼ cup (60 ml) of good cocoa powder.

How Much Frosting/Buttercream?

Size of cake	Butter	Confectioners' sugar
6 in (15 cm)	¼ cup (60 ml)	1 cup (250 ml)
7 in (18 cm)	⅓ cup (75 ml)	1⅓ cups (325 ml)
8 in (20.5 cm)	½ cup (125 ml)	1¾ cups (435 ml)
9 in (23 cm)	½ cup (125 ml)	1¾ cups (435 ml)
10 in (25.5 cm)	¾ cup (185 ml)	2½ cups (375 ml)
11 in (28 cm)	¾ cup (185 ml)	2½ cups (375 ml)
12 in (30.5 cm)	1 cup (250 ml)	3 cups (750 ml)

Basic frosting

This is a typical American recipe for a most delicious frosting. Although the technique is rather time-consuming in comparison to making buttercream, it is worth it. Bring all the ingredients to room temperature before you begin, and have the cake ready too.

INGREDIENTS
- **4 large eggs**
- **1 cup (250 ml) granulated sugar**
- **2 tsp (10 ml) vanilla extract or other flavoring**
- **½ tsp (2.5 ml) salt**
- **2 cups (500 ml) unsalted butter, cut into small, walnut-sized pieces**

1 In a glass mixing bowl, beat together the eggs, sugar, salt and vanilla extract.

2 Find a saucepan that the mixing bowl can straddle without touching the bottom. Pour about 1 in (2.5 cm) of water into the pan and bring to a boil. Reduce the heat to a simmer and place the mixing bowl over the water pot to form a double boiler. This will allow the eggs to heat up slowly and avoid them turning into scrambled egg.

3 Whisk continuously over the steaming water until the eggs reach 160°F (71°C) on a sugar thermometer.

4 Remove from the heat and beat the hot mixture until it cools to room temperature.

5 Beat in the butter one piece at a time until the frosting is smooth. Do not add the butter too quickly, otherwise the frosting will go thick and greasy. If the mixture starts to look curdled, continue to beat until smooth.

Buttercream

A traditional English recipe that uses equal quantities of butter and confectioners' sugar. For best results use a food mixer, although a wooden spoon will do too.

INGREDIENTS
- **1 cup (250 ml) unsalted butter, softened**
- **1¾ cups (435 ml) confectioners' sugar, sifted**
- **Flavoring (see Frosting Flavors, opposite)**

1 Place the butter in a glass bowl and add the sifted confectioners' sugar, a little at a time, beating slowly as you go. Add your chosen flavoring.

2 Once all the sugar has been incorporated, continue to beat until light and fluffy.

Storing Frosting

The frosting will last in the fridge for up to six days, or six months in a freezer. To reuse, make sure you warm the frosting up gradually, either over simmering water or in the microwave, beating as it starts to warm up. If you warm it up too quickly, put it back in the fridge for a while.

Storing Buttercream

Store buttercream in an airtight container and place in the fridge until required. Beat again before using. Buttercream can be stored in the refrigerator for up to two weeks.

pastes, icings, glues

There are various paste and frosting recipes
to choose from when decorating your cakes.

Modeling paste

Modeling paste is a malleable medium that
can be shaped, molded, crimped or textured to
within an inch of its life—and it will still keep its
shape. It is an excellent paste for a beginner to
start with. It dries slowly, so it can be worked
on for a great deal longer than either fondant
or gum paste, both of which will dry and crack
quickly. The gelatin in the paste means it sets
easily while remaining easy to work. Combined
with the gum tragacanth, a natural gum,
modeling paste is perfect for making finer
models. The paste is firm but stretchy and,
as you work it, the paste becomes easier to
shape and smoother, enabling you to crease
and texture without any cracking. Should the
paste get too dry, you can revive it a little by
adding more shortening.

Taste: The paste is not as sweet as fondant, but
still has a pleasant taste. The paste remains soft
inside after the outside has set firmly.

INGREDIENTS
- **1 rounded tsp (5 ml) gelatin**
- **1 tsp (5 ml) gum tragacanth**
- **1 rounded tsp (5 ml) shortening**
- **5 tsp (25 ml) cold water**
- **2¼ cups (225 g) confectioners' sugar**

1 Place the gelatin, gum tragacanth, shortening
and water in a small saucepan and heat gently until
the shortening and gelatin have dissolved and the
liquid is clear.

2 Gradually stir three-quarters of the confectioners'
sugar into the liquid until the mixture starts
coming together.

3 Tip out and knead in the remaining
confectioners' sugar (add a little more
confectioners' sugar if necessary) until the
paste is firm and pliable.

4 Place the paste in a plastic bag when not
in use as it will dry out and be unusable.

Storing Modeling Paste
Keep your paste sealed in a plastic bag or
plastic wrap when not in use to ensure it
doesn't dry out.

Gum tragancath and
fondant colored pink

Gum paste and fondant
colored yellow

Gum tragacanth

Gum tragacanth is a natural gum. It is a viscous, odorless, tasteless, water-soluble mixture of polysaccharides obtained from sap which is drained from the root of a Middle Eastern legume and dried. The gum seeps from the plant in twisted ribbons or flakes which can be powdered. It absorbs water to become a gel, which can be stirred into a paste. If you cannot find ready-made modeling paste, you can make your own by mixing food-grade gum tragacanth or tylose powder with fondant. It takes one hour to start working, but is even better left overnight.

INGREDIENTS
- **1 tsp (5 ml) gum tragacanth or 1 tsp (5 ml) tylose powder**
- **8 oz (225 g) fondant**

1 Sprinkle 1 tsp (5 ml) gum tragacanth or tylose powder onto your work surface.

2 Knead the fondant on the work surface until all the powder is incorporated.

3 Place in a plastic bag to "prove" for an hour. After an hour, it is usually firm enough to hold its shape.

Making Glue

To make a strong glue, sprinkle a few grains of gum tragacanth on top of a small amount of water. Allow it to sit for a while, then stir. At first it will clump together but then it will start to dissolve and the liquid will become thicker. Keep in a lidded container in the refrigerator and replace every 2–3 days.

Fondant and gum paste

An alternative to modeling paste is to use an equal amount of fondant and gum paste blended together. This will make a paste that can be worked in the same way as a modeling paste. It combines fondant, which by itself isn't capable of support, with gum paste. Gum paste is very stiff and requires kneading to soften, but by itself it sets solidly, which is fine for flowers that need to be textured, thinned, etc., but not for models.

Gum paste can be made from the recipe on page 30. It is used to make flowers but also for parts of a model that might require a little more support. If ready-made gum paste isn't available locally, follow the gum paste recipe and then add the same weight of fondant to make this variation of modeling paste.

Taste: This paste tastes much like fondant, except it is a little less sweet. The texture is slightly different with the addition of the gum paste. It will stay soft in the middle while the outside will dry.

Fondant
colored
yellow

Gum paste
colored peach

Fondant

Fondant and rolled fondant are the same thing—not to be confused with poured fondant—and are used to decorate cakes. This paste is made using gelatin (or agar in vegetarian recipes) and glycerin, which keep the sugar malleable and create a dough-like consistency, so it can be rolled out like pastry and used to cover cakes. This covering gives cakes a smooth, silky appearance.

Using store-bought fondant, which is available from specialty stores, saves time, and the consistency of the paste is constant and much less likely to crack and dry. If you prefer to make your own, or have difficulty obtaining fondant, this recipe makes 15½ cups (4 L).

Taste: A very sweet paste that, when added to the outside of cakes in a layer of approximately ⅓ in (1 cm), will complement the flavors in the cake. Sometimes it is necessary to use a thicker layer, but this may not enhance the overall taste of the cake. You may find that fondants made by different manufacturers taste slightly different. This is because they may have added taste enhancers.

INGREDIENTS
- **2 packets (8 tsp/40 ml) gelatin**
- **½ cup (125 ml) cold water**
- **2 tbsp (30 ml) glycerin**
- **1 cup (250 ml) liquid glucose**
- **15½ cups (4 L) confectioners' sugar, plus extra for dusting**

1 Sprinkle the gelatin over the cold water in a bowl and let it soak until it is spongy.

2 Stand the bowl over boiling water and stir until the gelatin dissolves.

3 Stir in the glycerin and glucose.

4 Sift 15½ cups (4 L) of the confectioners' sugar into a bowl and make a well in the center.

5 Slowly pour in the liquid, constantly stirring. Mix well.

6 Pour the fondant onto a work surface that has been well dusted with confectioners' sugar and knead until smooth.

Gum paste

Gum paste is a soft, malleable paste that sets very firmly when left to dry in air. It is perfect for making flowers because it holds its shape well, so it can be rolled out very thinly to make delicate petals or leaves. It is nonsticky and works well with molds and veiners.

Gum paste is available in various colors, although you can color the basic white and cream varieties using food colors.

Taste: Gum paste is not pleasant to eat by itself. As a soft paste it is slightly sweet but has a sticky texture. It does have confectioners' sugar in it, but it also has setting and gelling agents which give the paste its stretchy properties.

INGREDIENTS
- **1 lb (455 g) confectioners' sugar**
- **3 tsp (15 ml) gum tragacanth**
- **5 tsp (25 ml) cold water**
- **2 tsp (10 ml) powdered gelatin**
- **2 tsp (10 ml) shortening**
- **2 tsp (10 ml) liquid glucose**
- **1 large egg white**

Marzipan
colored
orange

1 Sieve the confectioners' sugar and gum tragacanth into a stainless steel electric mixer bowl. Use a strong electric mixer; this isn't the recipe for a handheld appliance.

2 Place the water in a pan and sprinkle the gelatin on the water. Leave to stand for 15–30 minutes. Warm gently until clear.

3 Add the shortening and liquid glucose to the gelatin mixture and warm until all three ingredients are clear and liquid.

4 Add the dissolved mixture and the egg white to the confectioners' sugar and beat using an electric mixer on a low speed until all the ingredients are blended together. The paste will look rather gray at this point, so don't panic.

5 Turn the electric mixer up to maximum, and beat the mixture until it becomes white and stretchy.

6 You will be able to tell when it is completed because the paste will go white. Place it in a plastic bag and into a plastic food container. Gum paste should be kept in the refrigerator. Allow to stand for 24 hours before using.

7 Pinch off small amounts at a time. Knead the paste to loosen it. The paste will become more malleable and smooth. If it's a little stiff, add a small amount of shortening to soften; if it's a little too sticky, add a small amount of confectioners' sugar. Add slowly, in very small amounts at a time.

Marzipan

Marzipan (or almond paste) is a soft, malleable paste that is used most frequently to cover a fruit cake before it is iced. It is primarily made from almonds and sugar, and is readily available from grocery stores. It is also a perfect medium for modeling, especially for the beginner, because it is easy to mold into an impressive model. A ready-made almond paste is good for modeling because it is a little firmer than most other marzipans and excellent at holding its shape. Softer marzipan is perfect for covering cakes, although nothing can beat the taste of homemade marzipan. When making your own paste, different flavors can be added to complement the cake flavor.

Taste: Marzipan has a grainy texture. It is sweet and has an almond flavor. It is very soft and the warmth of your hands will soften it further. If you model with homemade marzipan, you may find it too soft. Add a little gum tragacanth to it to make a firmer paste.

INGREDIENTS
- ¾ cup (185 ml) golden superfine sugar
- 2¼ cups (560 ml) confectioners' sugar, sifted, plus extra for dusting
- 5¼ cups (1.3 L) ground almonds
- Flavoring, such as the seeds from a vanilla pod or 2 tsp (10 ml) of rum (a little extra confectioners' sugar will be needed)
- 2 eggs, beaten

1 Place the sugars and ground almonds in a large bowl.

2 Rub in the vanilla seeds or add the rum.

3 Make a well in the middle of the bowl, add the eggs and blend using a knife.

4 Dust the work surface with confectioners' sugar and knead the marzipan to a smooth dough. Don't overdo the kneading since this will make the marzipan greasy. Add more confectioners' sugar if the paste becomes too sticky.

White modeling
chocolate
colored orange

Modeling chocolate

Like marzipan, modeling chocolate is an excellent medium to use for decorative models, from flowers on a wedding cake to animals on a birthday cake. It is available in three main colors: dark, milk and white. They are made from delicious Belgian chocolate and give a wonderful creamy flavor. The white modeling chocolate can be colored any shade you can imagine.

INGREDIENTS
- **8 oz (225 g) dark chocolate chips**
- **4 tbsp (60 ml) light corn syrup**

1 Melt the chocolate gently either over a double boiler on the stove top or in the microwave, giving it short bursts of 10 seconds, and then stirring until all is melted.

2 Add the corn syrup and blend. The mixture will start to become thicker and eventually become a ball of paste.

3 Place in a plastic bag and knead through the bag lightly. Place the chocolate in the refrigerator for a couple of hours.

Tips for Using Modeling Chocolate

- Don't knead it too much, since it will become very sticky and unusable.

- When adding color, blend for the shortest time possible, then leave in a plastic bag for a while to cool down and firm up.

- When making flowers or petals, roll the chocolate between two pieces of plastic—a plastic folder is ideal—to prevent the chocolate from becoming too warm and sticky, and to ensure there are no fingermarks.

- When softening modeling chocolate on a foam pad, press gently.

- Modeling chocolate will stick to itself without any glue or water to assist.

- Modeling chocolate will stay soft and malleable for a while, so pieces of the model will require support.

Royal icing

Royal icing is a hard white icing traditionally used on Christmas cakes and wedding cakes. When modeling, it can be used as an excellent "glue" to help attach large or heavy pieces. It can be textured into peaks, smoothed out to give a perfectly flat surface and piped into amazing shapes, such as coils, lines, shells and flowers, and is sometimes used for hair on figures.

Royal icing can be bought ready-made, but it is easy to make at home using a food mixer, confectioners' sugar and egg white or egg white substitute, with a little glycerin to stop it turning rock-hard. Egg substitute or fortified albumen, made into a liquid following the manufacturer's instructions, is a safer option than egg white, although the flavor is different.

Storing Royal Icing

Cover the surface of the icing with a damp sheet of paper towel or plastic wrap. This will stop the icing from crusting and blocking a piping tube. Royal icing lasts two days. Do not refrigerate unless placed in an airtight container.

INGREDIENTS
- **2 large egg whites or egg-white substitute made up following the manufacturer's instructions**
- **1¾ cups (435 ml) confectioners' sugar, sifted**
- **2 tsp (10 ml) glycerin**

1 First ensure the bowl of the food mixer is thoroughly clean and grease-free. Beat the egg liquid for one minute.

2 Add a tablespoon of confectioners' sugar at a time and beat in well.

3 Once all the sugar has been added, beat for a further minute, until sleek and shiny.

4 Add the glycerin and beat for a further minute.

5 Test the consistency of the icing. A cake coating needs to be softer than frosting for piping or decorative work in order to keep its shape.

Sugar sticks
These are made from gum paste and dried to use as supports in some models. If you don't have time to dry them, dry spaghetti is just as good. Although both sugar sticks and dry spaghetti are edible, sugar sticks are more tasty and should be used for children. For demonstration purposes, dry spaghetti is used throughout the topper directory.

INGREDIENTS
- **Gum paste**
- **½ tsp (2.5 ml) shortening**

1 Take a small amount of gum paste, add a little shortening and work it in to soften the paste.

2 Extrude through a clay gun with a medium-hole disk, making a long, thin string of paste.

3 Cut into long, medium and short lengths ready for different applications.

4 Dry flat on hard foam, rolling periodically to dry evenly.

Storing Sugar Sticks
Store sugar sticks in a cool, dry place, until required. If kept in a plastic bag, sugar sticks can be used indefinitely.

Edible glue
This quick and simple recipe makes an excellent glue for fixing parts of a model together. Ready-made edible glue can be purchased and works equally well. When making your own glue, ensure you use boiled water to remove any bacteria or fungus that might contaminate it and keep in a screw-topped jar. Apply using a clean paint brush.

INGREDIENTS
- **½ tsp (2.5 ml) gum tragacanth**
- **3 tbsp (45 ml) boiled water**

1 Sprinkle the gum tragacanth powder over the warm water and mix.

2 Leave until the powder is absorbed, then mix again. The mixture should be clear. The glue will be smooth, without lumps, and have a soft consistency. If the glue thickens or is too thick for your needs, add a little more boiled water.

Storing Edible Glue
Store in a screw-top jar. Use within a month.

preparing the cake

Preparing the cake should always come before you start to make your toppers, especially since in some cases the topper needs to be added to the cake before the topper dries, so that it can mold to the cake shape; for example, a figure sitting on the edge of a cake.

Leveling

Ideally, a cake with a depth of 3–3½ in (7.5–9 cm) is the perfect size to work with, because it allows for leveling without making the cake too shallow. The leveling process involves cutting away the domed top of the cake to give a nice flat surface.

Tools: Leveling

- Sponge cake (see pages 22–25)
- Tape measure
- Side scriber marker
- Long serrated knife
- Parchment paper
- Level
- Turntable (optional)

1 Measure the height of the side of the cake at its lowest point.

2 Set the height of the side scriber marker to this height and scribe a line all the way around the cake.

See also
Essential cake recipe, pages 22–25 > Cake frosting, pages 26–27 > Covering with frosting, pages 36–37

3 Use the long serrated knife to indent this line, and continue cutting deeper into the cake until the excess has been removed. Turn over so that the base is the top of the cake. This gives you a smooth surface that is flat and easy to cover.

4 Place parchment paper on the cake and the level on top of that to check that the cake is level. If it is not, carefully trim a little away from the raised point.

Filling

The delicious cake, carefully sliced (and perhaps sprinkled with syrup), is ready for filling. Follow the instructions on pages 26–27 to prepare your chosen filling of basic frosting or buttercream.

Tools: Filling

- Leveled sponge cake (see previous page)
- Cake drum
- Large and small palette knives
- Basic frosting or buttercream (see pages 26–27)
- Jam (optional)

1 Transfer the top layer of the cake (originally the base of the cake) to a spare cake drum and use a palette knife to spread frosting or buttercream over the cake, ensuring you spread evenly over the whole layer. If you are using it, spread jam over the filling.

2 Stack the top layer on top by sliding it gradually onto the layer of filling. If you are making a three-layer cake, then repeat the same filling process, remembering not to press too hard when spreading the filling.

Covering with frosting

Frosting, whether American frosting or buttercream, makes a delicious covering for a cake, and can be colored to match the theme of the celebration or its decoration. It can also be piped, swirled and textured.

The first application of frosting is known as a "crumb coat," and is a thin layer of frosting that sticks any loose crumbs to the cake, ensuring that the second and final layer is not spoiled by crumbs.

Tools: Covering with Frosting

- Filled sponge cake (see page 35)
- Basic frosting or buttercream (see pages 26–27)
- Palette knife
- Straight-edge ruler
- Decorating cake comb (see below)
- Large piping bag and decorating tip

1 Use the palette knife to spread the frosting thinly and smoothly over the top of the cake first, and then the sides of the cake. Place the cake in the refrigerator to chill.

2 Spread the next layer of frosting over the top of the cake. Draw the straight-edge ruler across the top of the cake, paddling back and forth, then scrape gently but smoothly in one direction to leave a smooth top. You can rechill and reapply if you want a thicker layer.

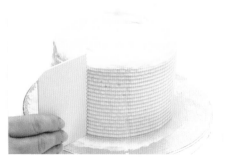

3 If you are using a cake comb to leave a pattern, use this now in the soft frosting and chill again.

4 Fill a large piping bag with a large decorating tip with frosting and pipe around the edge of the cake, covering the join. Pipe around the base of the cake also, if desired.

Covering with fondant

Covering a cake with fondant gives it a smooth, firm surface. Just before you are about to roll out the paste for cake covering, cover the cake again with a very thin layer of frosting, which will adhere the paste to the cake (see opposite).

Tools: Covering with Fondant

- Workboard
- Confectioners' sugar
- Fondant
- Large acrylic rolling pin
- Filled sponge cake (see page 35)
- Pin (optional)
- Palette knife
- Cake smoother

1 Dust the workboard with confectioners' sugar. Knead the fondant until it is soft and smooth. Roll out the paste to a thickness of around ¾ in (2 cm) using the rolling pin. Keep in mind the overall shape you require, rolling to approximately this shape.

2 Use the rolling pin to lift the paste onto the cake, making sure you have it positioned correctly. This method should prevent air getting trapped underneath the paste, which will cause a bubble in the frosting—if you do get a bubble, prick the hole with a fine pin and gently smooth the air out.

3 Start by smoothing with your hands to attach the paste to the cake. Roughly trim away excess paste with the palette knife. Use the cake smoother to smooth the top of the cake, then the sides. Trim further paste away neatly using the palette knife. Use the sharp edge of the cake smoother to give a neat finish to the base of the cake. Leave to dry.

4 If using marzipan, leave to dry for 24–48 hours. For fondant, continue by smoothing a pad of paste over the cake, paying particular attention to the edges. Smoothing with the pad will even out the surface, bring together any slight tears in the paste, and remove any stray grains of sugar.

color mixing

Color is hugely important when making cake toppers: it will make or break the cake. There is a huge range of coloring mediums on the market. They can be added to the basic pastes, paints and frostings before being used, or added later when the design has been completed. It is best to choose a slightly paler shade than the finished design. You can then use dusts or paints to accentuate and define sections of your topper, giving accents of light and shade and adding depth.

Color choice
Decide first whether you want a pastel effect with pale colors that are delicate, or bold, striking shades. Choose either harmonious or complementary colors. Harmonious colors are colors close together on the color wheel, while complementary colors are opposite each other on the wheel. Take purple and yellow—they look amazing together in a pastel shade or as bold colors. It is always better to make a color-test sketch first, so you can assess the overall effect. If you have particular shades that you need to match, perhaps for a particularly special cake, then you can blend colors together. It also makes a difference to the overall color if you use a powder color to color the paste rather than a liquid color or paste color.

Color strength
When adding color to paste, add it gradually, building up the strength of the color in the fondant. You can lighten the paste if you go too far by adding in some white fondant, which will dilute the color.

Types of Food Coloring

There are liquid colors, paste colors and petal dust colors. If you use chocolate modeling paste or marzipan, you will have to use a powder color, as liquid and paste colors makes these sticky and unworkable. Liquid color is good if you are making large volumes of one color. Weigh the paste and count the drops to ensure the same color every time. Paste colors are the easiest to use as they blend most quickly. If you are using a very dark color, wear gloves to prevent the color staining your hands.

NO COLOR: This disk shows the texture of the paste before coloring.

PASTE COLOR: These blend well into paste, creating a rich color.

LIQUID COLOR: This gives a smooth, slightly sticky result.

POWDER COLOR: This leaves a light grainy effect on the paste.

Make your own color mixes

You may want to match a fondant creation to a wedding scheme or sports team colors. The chart below is based on Wilton's Ready-to-Use Rolled Fondant and is © Wilton Industries, Inc (www.wilton.com, used with permission). Here, 4 oz (110 g) of fondant equals a 2½ in (6 cm) ball. Each mixture will produce 4–5 oz (110–140 g) of fondant.

2½ in (6 cm), 65% white + ¾ in (2 cm), 19% primary blue + ⅝ in (1.5 cm), 16% primary yellow = Aqua

2½ in (6 cm), 72% white + ½ in (1.2 cm), 14% natural dark brown + ½ in (1.2 cm), 14% primary yellow = Ivory

2½ in (6 cm), 83% neon yellow + ½ in (1.2 cm), 17% neon orange = Bright gold

2½ in (6 cm), 80% white + ½ in (1.2 cm), 16% neon purple + ⅛ in (0.3 cm), 4% primary blue = Lilac

2½ in (6 cm), 77% neon pink + ¾ in (2 cm), 23% natural black = Burgundy

2½ in (6 cm), 74% white + ⅝ in (1.5 cm), 19% neon pink + ¼ in (0.6 cm), 7% natural black = Mauve

2½ in (6 cm), 72% primary yellow + ½ in (1.2 cm), 14% primary red + ½ in (1.2 cm), 14% natural dark brown = Burnt orange

2½ in (6 cm), 80% primary blue + ⅝ in (1.5 cm), 20% natural black = Navy blue

2½ in (6 cm), 83% white + ½ in (1.2 cm), 17% natural black = Gray

2½ in (6 cm), 80% white + ½ in (1.2 cm), 16% primary green + ⅛ in (0.3 cm), 4% natural black = Sage green

Please note that the colors shown here are approximate and subject to the printing limitations.

Petal dusts

Petal dusts add shade and depth to dried icings and toppers. A dust can be added in small amounts to specific areas; for example, to deepen the color, highlight a petal or add pink cheeks to a figure, or it can be added over a large area to give the whole section a sparkle.

There are various dusts available on the Internet, including specialty luster, iridescent and metallic petal dusts. More than one luster dust can be used in the same area, whether harmonious or contrasting, to add further depth and realism to the design you are creating.

Tools

- Dry cake topper
- Paint brush
- Petal dust
- Paper towel

1 Load the paint brush with petal dust from the pot. Don't tip the dust directly from the pot as it may all drop out and be wasted.

2 Place the dust onto a piece of paper towel and work the dust into the brush.

3 Dust the intended spot with the loaded paint brush, taking care not to get dust onto any other part of the animal.

4 Build up the color with further layers of dust, rather than adding too much dust at one time.

Making a colored paint

Painting a color onto your topper, especially when using silver or gold, is best done using dust color and vodka (for an alcohol-free alternative, use water). The dust immediately turns to a liquid but dries almost instantly when applied to your topper.

Tools

- Dry cake topper
- Petal dust
- Palette
- Paint brush
- Vodka or water

1 Place a small amount of dust in the palette using a paint brush.

2 Add a few drops of vodka (or water) and mix with the dust to create a thin paste.

3 Apply to the topper using a paint brush. If the paint starts to thicken, add further drops of vodka.

4 Build up the color as you paint. You can apply both pale and dark colors to add detail and depth to the animal.

modeling techniques

Modeling with any medium requires a certain amount of skill. But the advantage of using modeling paste is that it gives you time to practice. If it doesn't look right, you can try again. Start with simpler models and build up confidence with them before moving on to the more complicated toppers. Each type of paste requires slightly different handling. Marzipan, for instance, takes less pressure to texture with the flower veining tool. This is the sort of experience you will build up the more you use the mediums.

Rolling paste

Modeling paste is straightforward to roll. It is soft and will not crack when rolled out; however, if you do keep rerolling the paste, it will ultimately dry out as it takes in the corn starch from the board. If this should happen, knead in a little shortening to moisten.

1 Lightly dust the workboard with the corn starch, then knead the paste a little to get a smooth surface to roll out.

Cutters are available in an inexhaustible supply, whether you are after standard shapes, such as circles, squares or hexagons, or coils, swirls or character cutters for any number of themes.

2 Roll out the chosen amount of paste carefully, using the rolling pin, rolling only a few times before moving the paste. This will ensure the paste does not stick to the board.

Shaping with fingers

Modeling with your fingers is one of those skills that will require practice. Start with simple shapes first to work out how to manipulate the paste. Get to know the feel of the paste and how much pressure is required to shape it. Marzipan, for instance, cannot be worked for too long as it gets warm and will not hold any shape.

Roll the paste into a ball and knead it to create a smooth paste that can then be shaped using your fingers. Naturally it lends itself to larger shapes such as heads or feet, but as you progress you will find you can even mold the fingers on a hand.

Shaping with tools

Many textures and shapes can be created using sugarcraft tools. The most varied and versatile is the clay gun. Different disks are inserted into the clay gun and these shape the paste into strings of different dimensions.

Start by softening the paste with a little shortening. If you don't do this you will never be able to squeeze the paste through the shaped disk at the end of the clay gun. The paste will still set. Insert the required disk, attach the end together, and then squeeze the handle to extrude the paste.

Cutting

When cutting, be sure not to pull the paste as this will either rip or crease it. Sometimes it is better to leave the paste for a minute or two to dry out a little, allowing for a neater and more professional cut.

The pizza cutter is possibly the best tool to use because it does not tempt you to pull the paste.

Paste cuts well with a knife. It is always best to use the sharpest knife you can in order to avoid tearing the paste.

Follow the same principle when using cutters as when cutting with a pizza cutter or knife, aiming to cut straight down without tearing the paste. Roll out only what you need to work with at the time and cover the remaining paste, otherwise it will dry too much.

Using modeling tools

There is an array of modeling tools on the market, but many are not essential, so don't buy anything until you are sure that it is something you will use frequently. Tools can be quite expensive. There are six major tools that are used in this book, which, along with the clay gun discussed on the previous page, are essentials. Plastic tools are lighter than their metal counterparts and, while they will eventually wear down, they are easy to manipulate.

Improvised Modeling Tools

There are many items to be found in any kitchen that work well for sugarcraft projects. Lollipop sticks are great for support but also for indenting nostrils; a glass-headed pin pushed into a cork makes a great ball tool; kitchen knives are invaluable, as is the pizza cutter.

Flower veining tool

The flower veining tool has a pointed end and a flatter, more rounded opposite end. The pointed end, as its name suggests, is for veining flowers. It leaves neat lines through the paste, which is perfect for marking creases. The flatter end can be used for smoothing paste or indenting mouths.

Small palette knife

Also known as the kemper knife, this mini palette knife has many uses. It has sharp sides which are very good for cutting paste and marking deep, sharp-edged grooves. It is also useful for applying small pieces of paste to a model.

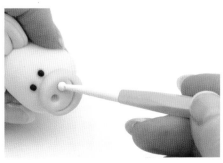

Tracing tool

This tool has two ends: one has a tiny, smooth wheel for running over a tracing or for free-hand indenting of paste; while the other has a tiny wheel that, when used on fresh paste, leaves a stitch effect which is perfect for marking neat edges to fabric or to create a "zipper" effect.

Ball tool

The ball tool has two different-sized balls at either end of the tool. It will make interesting indented patterns on fresh paste and features like nostrils or eye sockets.

Scallop tool

Another double-ended tool. One end has a semi-circle shape, ideal for creating fish scales or smiles; the opposite end of the tool has grooves that can be used to produce interesting impressions on fresh paste.

Bone tool

The bone tool has two different-shaped offset balls. They are excellent for smoothing and softening, texturing and making indentations such as mouths.

Attaching paste shapes

There are three possible techniques for attaching modeling paste. Sometimes it is necessary to use two methods to ensure the topper will not collapse.

Using edible glue

One method is to lightly brush one side of the two pieces to be attached with edible glue. A paint brush is adequate for this. The inexpensive equivalent of edible glue is water, but it is not as strong a fixative as edible glue.

Using royal icing

The second method is to use royal icing, which is a little stronger than water. Apply a few dots of royal icing using a brush or small spatula and press the pieces together for a few minutes, or until the icing begins to set.

Using sugar sticks

This technique is usually applied when larger, heavier pieces of paste are being joined. First push a sugar stick (or dry spaghetti) into one paste piece, then dab with edible glue or water...

... and push the two pieces together.

The weight of the puffin's head could not be supported by edible glue alone, and needs the extra internal support afforded by sugar sticks or dry spaghetti.

Creating texture

Adding texture to your models will make them look more realistic. It also disguises the joins. There are different textures that suit different animals—fur on a bear or feathers on a swan, for example. Texturing can also create a great border for your cake or topper.

The flower veining tool is the tool of choice to create creases at elbows or knees. Indent the soft paste with the sharper end of the tool and draw along the paste several times, creating different indentations.

A texture mat can be used to indent soft paste to give an overall effect. Texture mats are available to create different effects, from fur to flowers. The paste that you want to texture needs to be soft to achieve the best results.

For feathering, starting from the same point, use the flower veining tool to draw lines along the paste in the same direction in an ever-succeeding semicircle.

Score the paste using the small palette knife several times in the same direction. This will indent the paste and allow it to "kick up" a little, like little flecks of fur.

See also
Designing your figures, pages 48–51 > Designing a cake, pages 52–53

designing your figures

If you are new to fondant modeling, follow the step-by-step instructions. It will encourage you to concentrate on learning how to construct a cake topper, as well as improve your modeling skills and your design eye, without the worry of whether the model will work or the colors will go together. For the more experienced modeler, the challenge will come in designing and making your own model.

Designing your own figures

First draw a rough sketch of how you see the final cake coming together. This gives an idea of the pose, color and expression you want to create. The next step is looking for source material. This may be in the form of photographs, either from the internet or cut from magazines. You might have photographs, cards, labels and rough drawings in a drawer somewhere that you could rifle through to find some inspiration. A sketch of how the figures will interact with each other will take the worry out of the final construction. There is nothing worse than getting all your amazing models together and finding out that they just won't work on the cake. So plan ahead!

The Lion

The design decision here was for this lion to sit up rather than lay down. Its personality was serious. Unfortunately, it didn't work.

Good lion
The successful lion has a better nose, a more defined head shape, a contrasting colored mane and a smile—much more endearing than the first attempt.

Bad lion
Looking back on the original plan, it is obvious that the nose is out of proportion and that the hair isn't bushy enough.

Caricature
The eyes and muzzle of this panda needed to be accentuated a little to create the cartoon effect, but he too is a fine-looking topper.

Realistic
This is a more realistic panda. He is leaning back slightly, eating bamboo. It is a well-balanced cake topper and a really happy-looking panda.

The Panda
The panda on the right was made first. The standard black and white wasn't going to change, although perhaps he could have been made in different contrasting colors. Both toppers work.

Choosing a style
When planning toppers for your cake, you need to decide what style you want to make them in. If you are wanting a more realistic appearance for your animals, they must all be realistic. If you think a more caricatured appearance is more suitable, make sure the caricature style is consistently applied to all the toppers on the cake. It may be that you are more skilled in making cartoon/novelty toppers, or that the recipient loves a particular style.

Naturalistic
The realistic turtle, with its flippers curved backward swimming through the water, is a good example of a topper. The coloring on the head and shell add to the authenticity.

Expressive
The caricature turtle is brighter in color.

The Turtle
The turtle is sleek and fast in water, but slow on land. Here are the two alter egos of the turtle—one is swimming through the water, the other (a little more comical) is walking on land.

Expressive heads

There is only one feature altered in each case. Changing one feature gives the topper a completely different appearance. Altering facial features on animals can change them from simply being a basic animal to one that has more human features, possibly giving them a more comical/sad/surprised cartoon appearance.

Ears

Ears can give your topper an inquisitive streak. All three choices here are simple to create. Try combining two different variations.

A simple, triangular ear attached flat against the head, giving a fresh, open and natural look to the piggy face.

Add a deeper colored insert to the ear and texture to bend around slightly and the piggy now looks more alert. This is a higher quality of model, using two tones to add depth and interest.

Eyes

They say that eyes are the windows to the soul. So, what can you read from these three kitty heads? Eyes are very expressive, along with eyebrows, and, by adding a few creases, you can change simple, plain-looking eyes into ones that are smiling.

A simple expression that is a perfect start for a beginner.

These expressive eyes have a white eyeball and a pupil with a white dot that adds depth. The eyeball is teardrop shaped—this shape gives a slightly surprised/sad appearance.

Mouths

Mouths can be formed by simply indenting the paste using the back of a decorating tip. Just because you have decided to have an open mouth doesn't mean you need to have teeth. You can leave the area as it is, add in a block of black paste to fill the hole, put in one or two teeth, or add in a full set.

A simple mouth, made by indenting the paste with the end of a large decorating tip. You could also indent the ends of the mouth with the small end of the ball tool to give little dimples, or use a toothpick for the same effect.

The same decorating tip made this impression and, along with a few creases on the chin made using the flower veining tool, the cow is now miserable.

Creating expressive figures

For a beginner, learning the basic skills used to create toppers is difficult, but, as you improve and become more experienced, there needs to be a challenge involved in modeling cake toppers. Expression can be put into the animal by changing its position or adding props, but also by changing the facial expressions. Different-shaped eyes, noses, mouths, ears and even horns can all change the character of the topper. Each one of the three heads on the previous page has only one thing changed, but the difference it makes to the topper is fascinating. Consider the expression of your toppers before you start modeling and challenge yourself to add in expressions and bring your toppers to life.

A relaxed, floppy ear gives a very friendly appearance. The ear is made in the same way as the first head, but the ends of the ears have been softened and thinned. You can see this piggy relaxing in mud.

These eyes are rather feminine, with long lashes; a much fuller face with larger eyes showing a more open expression.

The flower veining tool was used to shape the lips and add a few creases. White paste was then pushed into the space, and the pointed end of the flower veining tool used to mark teeth.

Eyes
The eyes reinforce the impression of looking up and to the side. The dots of edible paint enliven the expression.

Head
The angle of the head, looking to the side and up, is very endearing.

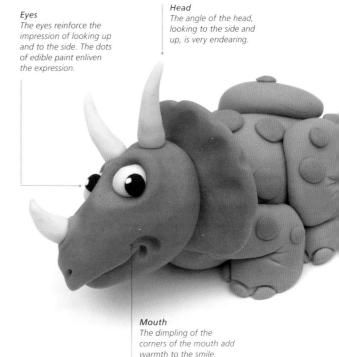

Mouth
The dimpling of the corners of the mouth add warmth to the smile.

designing a cake

It is important to consider design before making your cake. There are so many aspects to consider, from size, color, choice of toppers, their position and the suitability of the topper choices, be it a Christening or a 40th birthday party. As you can see, even cupcakes need to be considered in the same way to ensure that all your hard work is not wasted when you arrive at the most satisfying part of the project—putting everything together. Putting together an arrangement of toppers takes practice and creativity, but if you are willing to experiment in drawing first, it will be rewarding.

1 "Less is more." This is the most golden of all golden rules. A cake cluttered with all sorts of bits and pieces doesn't have the same impact as one that has fewer decorations. Don't clutter the cake so that none of your toppers can be appreciated.

2 Consider the size of the toppers and the size of the cake. There is nothing wrong with having a large topper on a small cake and a small topper on a large cake, but the latter will look a little lost unless some decoration or inscription is also included on the cake. It may be that you want a specimen topper, which is the focal point of the cake.

3 If you plan to have multiple toppers on the cake, the size of each one in comparison to the other must be well thought out. A huge zebra dwarfing a giraffe would not work on a cake.

4 Consider the intended mood of the cake. Do you want to create a comical cake with cartoon characters, or a more serious cake? This decision will give you a base to start your design.

5 Always remember the reason you are designing the topper. It may be for Thanksgiving, or a wedding where a specific theme has been decided. The appearance of the cake or cupcake should be as perfect as the topper.

6 Work carefully on the positioning of the toppers on the cake. Contemplate the pose of the toppers: sitting, standing, lying down? For a beginner, a sitting or lying pose would offer fewer complications. Draw out several different poses to see which would suit the occasion and the display.

This Thanksgiving cupcake has been beautifully presented in a stars-and-stripes case and accessorized with the addition of a flag.

These three butterflies look appealing balanced on the side of this cupcake. Their color could be adapted to suit any color scheme.

The flower details on the cupcake echo the flowers on the butterfly's wings and tie the topper and the cupcake together.

7 When drawing out your cake design and toppers, color them using colors you consider ideal for the occasion. It may be you have a specific color scheme to follow, perhaps for a wedding, so these colors are important and any additions to them should be either complementing or harmonizing. It may be that you have cupcake cases that you want to include. There is nothing wrong in using that color for your topper; make them the color that you feel will show them to their best advantage.

8 Choose appropriate props to go with your topper. Draw them into your design and assess their appropriateness both in appearance and size for inclusion in your cake design. You don't want them overshadowing your toppers.

9 When grouping toppers together, keep to odd numbers. The arrangement looks better balanced visually when there are 3, 5, 7 or 9 toppers. The organization of the toppers on the cake in this arrangement creates visual appeal.

10 Larger or taller toppers need to be correctly constructed so they don't collapse. Beginners who may be very enthusiastic to make the giraffe, for example, may struggle to support it sufficiently. If this is the case, use the side of the cake to support the topper.

Tall toppers, such as the giraffe, can be difficult to support. Either lean them against the side of a cake or just use the head to adorn a cupcake.

topper
directory

Choose one or more of your favorite animal toppers and follow the instructions on how to make them here.

01 crouching cat

This cat is crouching, ready to pounce. Remember to tell the recipient that you have used inedible wire for the whiskers.

Materials

- Modeling paste
- Corn starch
- Dry spaghetti
- Edible glue
- 24 ga. wire

Tools

- Workboard
- Rolling pin
- Flower veining tool
- Pizza cutter
- Paper towel

Colors Used

- 2¾ oz (78 g) gold
- ¾ oz (21 g) white
- ½ oz (14 g) cream
- Pinch black

Length: 3 in (8 cm)

See also
Pastes, icings, glues, pages 28–33 > Modeling techniques, pages 42–47 > Designing your figures, pages 48–51

6 For the bow, roll the cream paste into a sausage and flatten with the rolling pin. Use the pizza cutter to trim to a strip, cut in half, and fold over each to form a loop. Pinch the join together. Use rolled paper towel to support the loop until dry. Attach the loops to the head with edible glue and use the remnants of the paste to create a knot over the top of the join.

5 Roll a few tiny pinches of gold paste in the palm of your hand to make hair strands. Roll a sausage shape with points at either end, bend in half, and attach to the head using edible glue.

4 Shape the head from ½ oz (14 g) gold paste. Mold into a soft cone shape. Attach the broad end of the head to the body using the dry spaghetti and edible glue.

3 Shape the front legs from ¼ oz (7 g) gold paste. Shape into two elongated teardrops. Tuck the thin end under the head of the cat, securing with edible glue. Add two white front paws. Roll two pinches of white paste, flatten slightly, and attach to the front legs with edible glue. Indent the paws with the pointed end of the flower veining tool.

2 Make the back legs from ¼ oz (14 g) gold paste. Shape into two teardrops, flatten, and attach to the side of the abdomen using edible glue. Make two paws for the back legs as before.

1 Make the body from 1 oz (28 g) gold paste. Shape into an egg, then flatten the pointed end and insert dry spaghetti in preparation for the head.

7 Make the eyes from two tiny pinches of white paste. Shape into two teardrops and attach to the head with edible glue. Add two black pupils using half of the black paste.

8 Shape the muzzle from ¼ oz (7 g) white paste. Roll into two balls, flatten, and attach to the face with edible glue. Add a nose using the remaining half pinch of black paste. Shape it into a pyramid and attach to the muzzle using edible glue. Add a mouth with a pinch of white paste. Roll into a sausage that is flattened at either end. Attach to the underside of the muzzle using edible glue. Add short lengths of 24 ga. wire to the muzzle for whiskers.

9 Shape two pinches of gold paste into two teardrops for the ears. Flatten the center with the flat end of the flower veining tool, then attach to the head using edible glue. Add a tiny teardrop-shaped center to the ear using pinches of white paste.

10 Using the remaining gold paste, shape the tail into an elongated sausage that is thinner at one end. Tuck the thicker end under the abdomen and secure in place with edible glue. Hold the tail in position with a little paper towel until set.

02 sitting cat

Make this sitting kitty in any color you like.

Materials

- Modeling paste
- Corn starch
- Dry spaghetti
- Edible glue

Tools

- Workboard
- Rolling pin
- Flower veining tool

Colors Used

- 3 oz (84 g) mixed paste: 1½ oz (42 g) white, 1½ oz (42 g) lilac
- ½ oz (14 g) white
- Pinch pink
- Pinch blue
- Pinch black

Height: 3 in (8 cm)

See also
Pastes, icings, glues, pages 28–33 > Color mixing, pages 38–39 > Modeling techniques, pages 42–47

5 For the ears, roll out and cut triangles from a pinch of mixed paste. Attach with edible glue. Give the ears a little lining using tiny pinches of pale pink paste. Roll thinly and cut a smaller triangle. Attach as before.

6 Shape the eyes from tiny pinches of white, blue and black paste. Start with the white paste, roll into two balls and attach using edible glue. Do the same with the blue, then the black paste.

4 Add a nose made from a pinch of pink paste shaped into a triangle. Attach in the usual way.

3 Make the mouth and muzzle using ¼ oz (7 g) white paste. Pinch off a little for the mouth, then shape the remaining paste into two balls. Attach these to the face. Prick several times with the pointed end of the flower veining tool. Shape the pinch of white into a moon. Attach below the muzzle.

7 Shape the tail from ⅛ oz (4 g) mixed paste. Roll into a long thin sausage and tuck one end under the body, securing in place with edible glue.

2 Shape the head from ¾ oz (21 g) mixed paste. Roll into a ball and attach to the body with the dry spaghetti and a dab of edible glue.

1 For the body, shape 1 oz (28 g) mixed paste into a cone. Indent the tummy section to bend the cat over a little. Insert dry spaghetti through the neck for the head. Leave to dry.

8 For the big back leg, shape ¼ oz (7 g) mixed paste into a teardrop, flatten and bend the tip over slightly. Attach to the right hand side of the body. For the small leg on the left hand side, shape a pinch of mixed paste into a short sausage and tuck under the body. Attach with edible glue. Add a paw to each leg made from a pinch of white paste that has been indented with the pointed end of the flower veining tool.

9 To make the front legs, shape ½ oz (14 g) mixed paste into a long sausage and cut in two. Attach to the front of the cat with edible glue. Make two paws as before.

03 chihuahua

This inquisitive little creature—the smallest breed of dog—is sure to impress any dog-lover.

Materials

- Modeling paste
- Corn starch
- Edible glue
- Dry spaghetti

Tools

- Workboard
- Rolling pin
- Flower veining tool
- Ball tool

Colors Used

- 5⅛ oz (145 g) light brown
- ¼ oz (7 g) white
- Pinch dark brown
- Pinch black

Height: 6 in (15 cm)

See also
Pastes, icings, glues, pages 28–33 > Modeling techniques, pages 42–47 > Designing your figures, pages 48–51

6 Add a streak of white hair between the ears using a pinch of white paste, rolled into a cigar shape. Flatten, texture with the flower veining tool, and attach to the head with edible glue.

7 Shape the eyes from two large balls of black paste. Insert into the eye sockets and secure in place with edible glue.

5 Shape ears from ½ oz (14 g) light brown paste. Shape into two ovals, but thin around the edges. Cut off one curved end and attach to the head with edible glue. Support for a few seconds.

8 Roll ⅛ oz (4 g) white paste into two balls and attach to the face with edible glue to create cheeks. Shape the dark brown paste into a triangle for the nose and secure in place with edible glue. Roll a tiny pinch of light brown paste into a cigar shape for the mouth, and attach with edible glue.

4 Shape 1 oz (28 g) light brown paste into a domed ball for the head. Indent the eye sockets using the larger end of the ball tool. Attach to the body using edible glue and dry spaghetti.

1 Mold 2 oz (58 g) light brown paste into an elongated egg. Stand on the broader end of the shape.

3 Shape the back legs from 1 oz (28 g) light brown paste. Roll into two thick sausages. Flatten one end, then bend at the knee area and the ankle area. Create paws as you did in Step 2. Attach to the body with edible glue, allowing the legs to flop to either side in a relaxed fashion.

2 Roll ½ oz (14 g) light brown paste into two little sausages. Narrow at one end and indent the narrower end using the flower veining tool to represent paws. Attach to the shoulders using edible glue, allowing the paws to bend at the wrist.

04 dalmatian

Increase or decrease the number of spots to personalize this adorable pup.

Materials
- Modeling paste
- Corn starch
- Edible glue
- Dry spaghetti

Tools
- Workboard
- Rolling pin
- Small palette knife
- Flower veining tool

Colors Used
- 3½ oz (98 g) white
- 1 oz (28 g) black
- Pinch pink

Height: 3½ in (9 cm)

See also
Pastes, icings, glues, pages 28–33 > Modeling techniques, pages 42–47 > Designing your figures, pages 48–51

6 Make both ears from about ⅛ oz (4 g) of white paste. Shape into two teardrops, flatten and bend over a little at the narrower end. Attach to the head using edible glue.

5 Shape the head into a cone using ⅝ oz (18 g) of white paste. Flatten slightly, then attach to the body using dry spaghetti and edible glue.

4 Roll a pinch of white paste into a long sausage shape for the tail. Curl one end around and tuck the other end under the base of the body, securing in place with edible glue.

3 Take ⅜ oz (11 g) of white paste for the back legs, roll into a small cone, indent the front as before with the flower veining tool, and attach to the side of the body with edible glue.

7 Shape the muzzle from a pinch of white paste. Roll into a ball, then indent firmly with the flower veining tool. Attach to the face using edible glue. Make the eyes from tiny pinches of black paste rolled into a ball, and secure into place on the face. Shape the tongue from a pinch of pink paste, shape into a teardrop, flatten with the flower veining tool and attach to the mouth by pushing the point of the teardrop just under the muzzle. Secure in place using edible glue.

2 Roll two ⅛ oz (4 g) balls of white paste for the front paws. Flatten the balls slightly, then indent the front edge with the flower veining tool to shape them further. Attach in place to the front of the body using edible glue.

1 Shape the body from 1⅛ oz (32 g) white paste, shape into a softened cone, flattening the top. Indent the top with the small palette knife to shape the front legs. Use the flower veining tool to accentuate the indentation.

8 Make the spots and the foot pads using tiny pinches of black paste. Roll into balls and flatten, securing into place using edible glue.

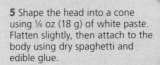

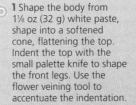

05 west highland terrier

Add a ball of fondant paste to the top of your cake to create a toy for this playful character.

Materials

- Modeling paste
- Corn starch
- Edible glue
- Dry spaghetti

Tools

- Workboard
- Rolling pin
- Flower veining tool
- Bone tool
- Pizza cutter
- Paper towel
- Ball tool

Colors Used

- 3¼ oz (92 g) white
- Pinch green
- Pinch pale pink
- Pinch dark pink
- Pinch black

Length: 3½ in (9 cm)

See also
Pastes, icings, glues, pages 28–33 > Modeling techniques, pages 42–47 > Designing your figures, pages 48–51

3 Shape 1 oz (28 g) white paste into a cone for the head. Push the narrow end down slightly for the nose. Indent eye sockets with the bone tool. Mark the muzzle and mouth with the flower veining tool. Attach the head on top of the forelegs and body using dry spaghetti and edible glue. Score the head to represent fur.

2 For the forelegs roll ½ oz (14 g) white paste into two sausages that are thinner at one end. Mark the broader end using the flower veining tool to texture the paws. Attach to the head end using edible glue. Score the paws, as before, to give the impression of fur.

1 Shape 1 oz (28 g) white paste into a teardrop for the body. Flatten the point and thin the pointed end. Score the body using the flower veining tool to represent fur.

4 For the ears roll ⅛ oz (4 g) white paste into two teardrops and flatten the center using the flat end of the flower veining tool. Shape to a point, trim the opposite end flat, and attach to the head using edible glue.

5 Roughly blend pinches of green, pale pink, dark pink and white pastes. Roll into a long sausage and flatten. Trim to approximately 2 x ¼ in (5 x ½ cm) using the pizza cutter. Loop the short edges to the middle and secure in place with edible glue. Support the loops with rolls of paper towel (remove when dry). Cover the join of the loops with a strip of left-over blended paste. Attach the bow to the head using edible glue.

6 Roll two tiny eyes from the black paste and secure in place using edible glue. Make the nose from the remaining black paste. Shape into a pyramid and use the small end of the ball tool to mark the nostrils in the nose. Attach with edible glue.

7 For the back legs roll ½ oz (14 g) white paste into two teardrops, and flatten the body of the teardrop, shaping the thinner section into the back paw. Shape the paw end using the flower veining tool. Attach to the body using edible glue. Score the legs with the flower veining tool to represent fur.

9 Finish the terrier by rolling pinches of white paste to form thin sausages, flatten, and score with the pointed end of the flower veining tool, working across the paste to give a furry texture. Attach to the face, either side of the nose and across the top of the head, using edible glue.

8 Shape the tail from ⅛ oz (4 g) white paste. Roll into a teardrop, and score from the broad to narrow end using the flower veining tool to create texture. Attach to the body using edible glue and dry spaghetti to keep the tail upright.

06 boxer

Change this dog's expression by raising or lowering his eyebrows.

Materials

- Modeling paste
- Corn starch
- Edible glue
- Dry spaghetti

Tools

- Workboard
- Rolling pin
- Flower veining tool
- Bone tool
- Paper towel

Colors Used

- 4¾ oz (132 g) mixed paste: 2¼ oz (62 g) chestnut, 2½ oz (70 g) white
- ½ oz (14 g) white
- Pinch black

Height: 3½ in (9 cm)

See also
Pastes, icings, glues, pages 28–33 > Color mixing, pages 38–39 > Modeling techniques, pages 42–47

4 For the eyebrows, roll two tiny pinches of mixed paste into sausages and attach to the head using edible glue.

3 Use 1 oz (28 g) mixed paste for the head. Shape into a rough cone, but flatten the point. Indent the eye sockets using the small end of the bone tool. Attach to the body using dry spaghetti and edible glue.

2 Shape the front legs from 1 oz (28 g) mixed paste. Shape into two sausage shapes, then thin one end for the paws. Attach to the front of the body with edible glue, then indent the paws using the pointed end of the flower veining tool.

1 Make the body from 2 oz (56 g) mixed paste. Shape into a cone and soften the edges.

5 The ears are made from ¼ oz (7 g) mixed paste, rolled into two teardrops. Flatten the center to form a rough triangle and secure to the head with edible glue. Bend the ears forward slightly and support in place with rolled paper towel until set.

6 Roll two tiny pinches of white paste into balls for the eyes and attach using edible glue. Add two tiny pupils from pinches of black paste.

7 Make the muzzle from ¼ oz (7 g) white paste. Roll into two balls and flatten slightly to make two ovals. Attach with edible glue. Add a sliver of white paste to the underside of the muzzle for the mouth with edible glue.

8 Make a nose from the remaining black paste, shaped into a pyramid. Attach with edible glue.

9 Shape the tail from a pinch of mixed paste. Roll into a long thin sausage, flatten the end, and secure to the dog using edible glue.

10 Finish by adding the back legs. Shape ¼ oz (7 g) mixed paste into two sausages, flatten one half, and attach this to the body with edible glue. Indent with the flower veining tool to represent back paws.

07 dachshund

This little guy has the characteristic long body and short legs of the sausage dog.

Materials

- Modeling paste
- Corn starch
- Edible glue
- Dry spaghetti

Tools

- Workboard
- Rolling pin

Colors Used

- 2 oz (56 g) brown
- Pinch black

Length: 2¾ in (7 cm)

See also
Pastes, icings, glues, pages 28–33 > Modeling techniques, pages 42–47 > Designing your figures, pages 48–51

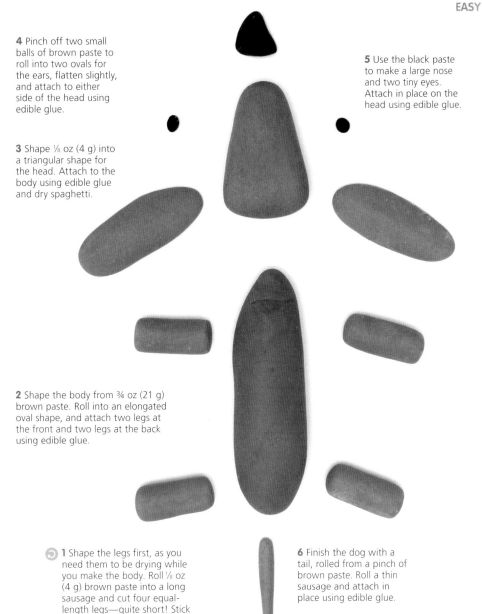

4 Pinch off two small balls of brown paste to roll into two ovals for the ears, flatten slightly, and attach to either side of the head using edible glue.

5 Use the black paste to make a large nose and two tiny eyes. Attach in place on the head using edible glue.

3 Shape ⅛ oz (4 g) into a triangular shape for the head. Attach to the body using edible glue and dry spaghetti.

2 Shape the body from ¾ oz (21 g) brown paste. Roll into an elongated oval shape, and attach two legs at the front and two legs at the back using edible glue.

1 Shape the legs first, as you need them to be drying while you make the body. Roll ⅛ oz (4 g) brown paste into a long sausage and cut four equal-length legs—quite short! Stick the legs together in groups of two lengthwise so you have two pairs. Leave to dry.

6 Finish the dog with a tail, rolled from a pinch of brown paste. Roll a thin sausage and attach in place using edible glue.

guinea pig

You could color your fondant guinea pig to match your pet.

Materials

- Modeling paste
- Corn starch
- Edible glue

Tools

- Workboard
- Rolling pin
- Flower veining tool
- Ball tool
- X-acto knife

Colors Used

- 1¼ oz (35 g) light brown
- 1 oz (28 g) black
- 1 oz (28 g) white
- 1 oz (28 g) medium brown
- 1 oz (28 g) dark brown
- ½ oz (14 g) pink

Length: 4 in (10 cm)

See also
Color mixing, pages 38–39 > Modeling techniques, pages 42–47 > Props, pages 248–253

4 Shape a muzzle using a pinch of light brown paste. Roll into a ball and cut in half using the X-acto knife. Attach to the face and prick with the pointed end of the flower veining tool. Attach a triangle of pink paste for the nose.

3 Roll two large pinches of light brown paste into two balls for ears. Indent the center with the ball tool, and attach to the head using edible glue. Smooth the base of the ear to blend with the head.

2 Shape 1 oz (28 g) light brown paste into an oval for the head. Use the flower veining tool to texture. Attach to the body and finish the texturing so the paste stretches over the body.

1 Shape the body using the black (leave a pinch for the eyes), white (leave a pinch for the teeth), medium-brown and dark brown pastes. Roll each into a ball, then combine the balls into an oval—but don't over work them, as you want them to stick together but not blend too much. Score down the body with the flower veining tool to give the impression of fur.

5 For the mouth, mold a cigar shape from a pinch of light brown paste and attach beneath the muzzle with edible glue. Roll out and flatten the remaining white paste. Cut into a rectangle, pinch one end, and cut a "v" in the other end. Attach to the mouth with edible glue to create two front teeth.

6 Shape the eyes from the remaining black paste, securing in place with edible glue.

7 The back paws are shaped from ¹/₈ oz (7 g) pink paste. Roll into two teardrops, flatten slightly, and indent with the flower veining tool. Attach to the side of the body. Shape the remaining pink paste into two teardrops, flatten and, using the X-acto knife, cut out three triangles. Tuck the front paws under the head, securing with edible glue.

09 hamster

This hamster is storing lots of food in his bulging cheeks.

Materials
- Modeling paste
- Corn starch
- Edible glue
- Edible white paint
- Royal icing

Tools
- Workboard
- Rolling pin
- Flower veining tool
- Ball tool
- Small palette knife
- Paint brush

Colors Used
- 5½ oz (154 g) yellow
- Pinch white
- Pinch black
- Pinch pink
- Pinch orange (optional)

Height: 4 in (10 cm)

See also
Pastes, icings, glues, pages 28–33 > Modeling techniques, pages 42–47 > Props, pages 248–253

6 Roll a pinch of white modeling paste into two balls for the eyeballs. Do the same with black paste, and attach with edible glue. Add a tiny white dot of edible white paint to the pupil.

7 Add a nose to the figure using the pink modeling paste. Secure with edible glue.

8 If you wish, make a carrot from orange paste. Roll into a short sausage then indent with the flower veining tool and secure in the hands using edible glue.

5 Roll ½ oz (14 g) yellow paste into two balls and indent with the ball tool to create ears. Attach to the head using edible glue.

4 Roll ½ oz (14 g) yellow paste into a "space ship" shape to create the head and chubby cheeks. Indent the eye sockets with the smaller end of the ball tool. To create the mouth, push the small end of the ball tool into the paste, then upward to bulge the upper lip section. Use the small palette knife to indent the bulge in an upward direction toward the nose, then use the flower veining tool to define each side of the mouth.

9 To finish, paint the muzzle of the face with a little royal icing and score with the pointed end of the flower veining tool.

3 Shape the front paws from ½ oz (14 g) yellow paste. Roll into a thin sausage and cut in half. Flatten one end and use the flower veining tool to mark the paws. Attach the paws to the shoulders of the body, allowing the arms to rest on the top of the back legs.

2 For the back legs, roll 2 oz (56 g) yellow paste into two elongated teardrops. Bend the narrower ends over. Attach to the sides of the body using edible glue.

1 For the body, shape 2 oz (56 g) yellow paste into a ball.

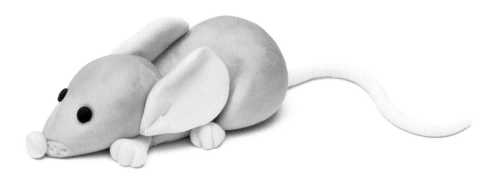

mouse

This sweet, simple mouse is very easy to make, so is great for beginners.

Materials

- Modeling paste
- Corn starch
- Edible glue
- Dry spaghetti
- Light brown petal dust

Tools

- Workboard
- Rolling pin
- Bone tool
- Small palette knife
- Flower veining tool
- Dusting brush

Colors Used

- 3 oz (84 g) light brown
- 1 oz (28 g) pale pink
- Pinch black

Length: 2¾ in (7 cm)

See also
Pastes, icings, glues, pages 28–33 > Color mixing, pages 38–39 > Modeling techniques, pages 42–47

7 Use the brush to lightly dust the top of the mouse head and body with the petal dust, building up the color until you are satisfied.

6 Finish the mouse with two tiny black eyes made from the black paste and add a tiny pink ball to the end of the snout for the nose. Attach to the head with edible glue.

5 The ears are made from ¼ oz (7 g) pink paste. Roll the paste out thinly, cut out two petal shapes and gently pinch the pointed end together. Attach to the head with edible glue.

4 For the paws, make four equal teardrops from ¼ oz (7 g) pink paste. Indent the paws using the pointed end of the flower veining tool. Attach to the body using edible glue.

1 Shape the head from 1 oz (28 g) light brown paste. Mold into an egg shape, then thin down the narrower end for the nose. Indent the paste using the end of the bone tool for the eye sockets and mark the mouth and nose using the small palette knife. Prick the muzzle section with the end of the flower veining tool to represent the whiskers.

2 Shape the body from 2 oz (56 g) light brown paste. Shape in the same way as the head. Indent either side of the abdomen using the flower veining tool to mark the back legs. Attach to the head using dry spaghetti and edible glue.

3 Make the tail from ½ oz (14 g) pink paste. Roll into a long thin sausage, narrowing to a fine end. Attach to the back of the abdomen using edible glue.

rabbit

This rabbit would be a great addition to an Easter or spring cake.

Materials

- Modeling paste
- Corn starch
- Edible glue
- Dry spaghetti

Tools

- Workboard
- Rolling pin
- Flower veining tool
- Paper towel
- Bone tool

Colors Used

- 3½ oz (98 g) gray
- ¾ oz (21 g) white
- ¼ oz (7 g) pink
- Pinch blue
- Pinch black

Height: 2¾ in (7 cm)

See also

Pastes, icings, glues, pages 28–33 > Modeling techniques, pages 42–47 > Designing your figures, pages 48–51

6 Make the cheeks from ¼ oz (7 g) white paste. Roll into balls, flatten slightly, and prick several times with the end of the flower veining tool. Attach to the face using edible glue.

5 Make the eyes by rolling two pinches of white paste into two teardrops. Attach to the face with edible glue. Add two tiny blue balls of paste, flattened slightly, again securing in place with edible glue. Add a tiny black pupil to each, securing as before.

4 For the ears, shape ¾ oz (21 g) gray paste into two teardrops and indent the center using the flattened end of the flower veining tool. Roll a pinch of pink paste into a teardrop and secure in the ear using edible glue. Attach the ears to the head with edible glue and support in shape until dry.

3 Roll the head from ½ oz (14 g) gray paste. Shape into a cone, flattening one side to broaden the muzzle section. Indent the eye area.

2 For the chest, roll out ⅛ oz (4 g) white paste into a rough oval. Mark the fur using the pointed end of the flower veining tool. Attach to the body using edible glue.

1 Shape the body from 1 oz (28 g) gray paste. Shape into a cone, flatten the top slightly, and insert dry spaghetti through the neck for the head.

7 The nose is made from a pinch of pink paste shaped into a tiny pyramid and attached with edible glue.

8 Shape the front paws from ½ oz (14 g) gray paste, rolled into two teardrops. Flatten the broad end slightly and indent with the pointed end of the flower veining tool for the paws. Attach around the top part of the body using edible glue. Hold in place with a paper towel until dry.

9 Roll a tiny ball of white paste, elongate slightly, and flatten the narrower end. Indent the ball several times with the end of the bone tool to create a fluffy effect. Tuck the flattened end under the body and secure with edible glue.

10 Shape the back paws from ½ oz (21 g) gray paste. Roll into teardrops. Flatten slightly at the narrow end and bend the broader section up to create a foot. Indent the end of the paws using the pointed end of the flower veining tool. Finish the base of the paws by adding three small flattened balls of white paste.

12 rooster

Cock-a-doodle-doo! Luckily, this rooster won't wake you up in the morning.

Materials

- Modeling paste
- Corn starch
- Dry spaghetti
- Edible glue
- Black edible paint

Tools

- Workboard
- Rolling pin
- Flower veining tool
- X-acto knife
- Paint brush

Colors Used

- 4⅛ oz (116 g) white
- ⅛ oz (4 g) black
- ⅛ oz (4 g) red
- Pinch yellow
- Pinch gray

Length: 3½ in (9 cm)

See also
Pastes, icings, glues, pages 28–33 > Color mixing, pages 38–39 > Modeling techniques, pages 42–47

3 Shape the beak from the yellow paste. Make a cone shape, accentuating the point. Use the X-acto knife to mark a line down each side of the beak and attach to the face with edible glue.

2 Shape the head from 1 oz (28 g) of white paste. Shape into a cone and flatten the top and bottom, feathering out the bottom with the flower veining tool. Texture the length of the head and neck with the flower veining tool.

1 Shape the body from 2 oz (56 g) white paste. Shape into a long teardrop. Flatten the shape sideways along where the wings will be. Flatten the tail end and raise up slightly. Use the flower veining tool to mark lines along the sides of the body and along the tail. Push some dry spaghetti into the fatter section ready for the head.

4 Take two pinches of black paste to form the eyes and attach to the head with edible glue.

5 Use half the red paste to make the wattle. Shape into a flattened teardrop, texture with the flower veining tool, and secure under the beak with edible glue.

6 With the remaining red paste, make the comb. Shape into a sausage and flatten. Using the X-acto knife, cut out triangular sections from one long side. Pinch these together to make them more pointed. Curve the comb into a kidney shape and attach to the head using edible glue.

7 Mark the base of the neck with a fairly dry paint brush loaded with black edible paint to give a mottled effect.

9 Roll black, white and gray pinches of paste into sausage shapes, flatten them and texture with the flower veining tool to represent the long tail feathers of the cockerel. Attach to the tail with edible glue.

8 Take ½ oz (14 g) of white paste for each wing, shape into a teardrop and flatten. Use the flower veining tool to draw lines from the broad end to the narrower end, allowing the lines to go over the edge. Attach to the side of the body with edible glue.

COW

Use this cow with props such as the fence and the feeding trough to make a farmyard-themed cake.

Materials

- Modeling paste
- Corn starch
- Edible glue
- Dry spaghetti

Tools

- Workboard
- Rolling pin
- Flower veining tool
- Bone tool
- Ball tool

Colors Used

- 4 oz (112 g) white
- 1 oz (28 g) pink
- ¾ oz (21 g) black

Length: 2¼ in (6 cm)

See also
Pastes, icings, glues, pages 28–33 > Designing your figures, pages 48–51 > Props, pages 248–253

4 Make the nose from the pink paste, but first take two pinches off for the ears. Roll the rest into a ball, flatten, then indent the nostrils using the pointed end of the flower veining tool. Mark the mouth with the flower veining tool, then indent each end with the small end of the ball tool. Attach to the head with edible glue and dry spaghetti.

5 Make the eyes from two tiny pinches of black paste, and attach into the indentations you made earlier using edible glue.

6 Shape the ears from the pinches of pink paste you saved from the nose. Roll into two balls, then into a teardrop shape. Flatten with the end of the flower veining tool. Pinch the pointed end together and cut off the point to flatten. Attach to the head using edible glue.

3 Form the head from ½ oz (14 g) white paste. Shape into an egg, then flatten the more pointed end. Indent for the eyes using the smaller end of the ball tool. Attach to the body with edible glue and dry spaghetti.

7 Shape the horns from two pinches of white paste. Shape into a cone in the palm of your hand, then curve the point slightly. Attach to the head using edible glue.

2 Shape the hooves from ½ oz (14 g) black paste. Shape into triangular blocks.

1 For the body, roll 3 oz (84 g) white paste into a large egg shape. Indent at each side and at the front and back, using the flower veining tool to give the impression of legs.

8 Take various pinches of black paste, flatten into different-sized shapes, and attach to the cow with edible glue.

14 donkey

A quietly unassuming donkey.

Materials

- Modeling paste
- Corn starch
- Edible glue
- Dry spaghetti
- Shortening

Tools

- Workboard
- Rolling pin
- Flower veining tool
- X-acto knife
- Clay gun

Colors Used

- 3⁵/₈ oz (102 g) gray
- 1⅛ oz (32 g) black
- ¾ oz (21 g) cream

Height: 4 in (10 cm)

See also
Pastes, icings, glues, pages 28–33 > Modeling techniques, pages 42–47 > Props, pages 248–253

6 Make the ears from ¼ oz (7 g) gray paste. Roll thinly and, using the X-acto knife, cut two triangles. Attach to the head using edible glue. Add two small cream triangles inside the ears, attaching in the usual way.

5 Roll two tiny pinches of black paste into balls for the eyes. Attach to the head using edible glue.

4 Make the nose from ½ oz (14 g) cream paste. Roll into a cylinder, soften one end, and narrow slightly. Attach to the head using edible glue and dry spaghetti. Mark the nose with the flower veining tool.

3 Shape the head from 1 oz (28 g) gray paste. Roll into a cylinder that is slightly fatter in the middle. Cut off one end, about one quarter of the way down. Indent eyes. Attach to the body using edible glue and dry spaghetti.

2 Shape the body from 2 oz (56 g) gray paste. Roll into a ball. Attach the feet to the ball using edible glue and dry spaghetti.

7 The mane is made from ¼ oz (7 g) gray paste and ¼ oz (7 g) cream paste roughly mixed together. Add shortening to soften, then extrude the paste through the clay gun with the multihole disk. Attach the mane using edible glue.

8 Use ⅛ oz (4 g) gray paste to make the tail. Roll into a long, thin sausage. Score one end to texture for the tassel of the tail. Attach to the bottom of the donkey using edible glue.

1 Make the hooves using 1 oz (28 g) black paste. Shape into four short cylinders. Allow to dry.

goat

Make two more goats and he will be one of the three billy goats gruff.

Materials

- Modeling paste
- Corn starch
- Dry spaghetti
- Edible glue
- Black petal dust
- Pink petal dust

Tools

- Workboard
- Rolling pin
- Decorating tip No. 1
- Flower veining tool
- Ball tool
- Dusting brush

Colors Used

- 4½ oz (126 g) white
- ½ oz (14 g) brown
- Pinch black

Height: 3½ in (9 cm)

See also
Pastes, icings, glues, pages 28–33 > Color mixing, pages 38–39 > Modeling techniques, pages 42–47

4 For the horns, shape ⅛ oz (4 g) white paste into two balls, then into teardrops. Twist the teardrops to coil slightly but keep the length. Attach to the head using edible glue and support until dry. Dust with black petal dust to give a slightly gray color.

5 For the ears, roll out ⅛ oz (4 g) white paste and cut a round disk using the end of the flower veining tool. Cut in half, then soften both halves with the flat end of the flower veining tool to lengthen. Attach to the head using edible glue, support until dry, and dust lightly on the back with black petal dust and inside with pink petal dust.

3 For the head, shape 1 oz (28 g) white paste into a rough cone and soften the points. Pinch in slightly below the top of the cone to elongate the "nose" section. Indent the mouth using the end of the decorating tip. Indent the eye sockets using the small end of the ball tool. Add in eyes using two balls of black paste and secure with edible glue.

6 For the beard, roll a pinch of white paste into a teardrop and, using the pointed end of the flower veining tool, score several times, drawing down to the point. Secure using edible glue.

2 For the body, shape 2 oz (56 g) white modeling paste into a large cone. Using the flower veining tool, score down the body to create a texture that will resemble fur. Attach to the legs with a little edible glue and the dry spaghetti. Push dry spaghetti in the top, ready to support the head.

7 Shape the nose from a pinch of white paste. Use the flower veining tool to indent a triangle and attach using edible glue. Lightly dust pink petal dust on the nose and cheeks.

1 For the hooves, roll out the brown paste and cut four circles using the end of the decorating tip. Shape the legs from 1 oz (28 g) white paste. Split into four balls, and roll into cones with the base the same diameter as the hooves. Stick the brown circles to the bottom of the cones using edible glue. Insert dry spaghetti into the top of each leg and leave to dry.

8 Make the tail from a pinch of white paste. Roll into a teardrop, then, using the pointed end of the flower veining tool, score down one side. Attach the broad end to the body using edible glue, supporting until dry.

horse

This horse is saddled and ready to top a riding enthusiast's cake.

Materials

- Modeling paste
- Corn starch
- Dry spaghetti
- Edible glue
- Shortening

Tools

- Workboard
- Rolling pin
- Decorating tip No. 1
- Ball tool
- Flower veining tool
- X-acto knife
- Pizza cutter
- Tracing wheel
- Clay gun

Colors Used

- 3½ oz (98 g) brown
- ½ oz (14 g) black
- ⅛ oz (4 g) white
- Pinch orange

Height: 4½ in (11 cm)

See also
Color mixing, pages 38–39 > Modeling techniques, pages 42–47 > Props, pages 248–253

4 For the head, roll ½ oz (14 g) brown paste into a teardrop. Cut the narrow end off and flatten the broader end slightly. Add a couple of pinches of white paste to the cutoff brown paste, blend, and shape into a muzzle. Attach to the narrower end using edible glue. Leave to dry for 15 minutes. Dab edible glue onto the dry spaghetti in the neck and push the spaghetti into the head to attach. Support until dry. Indent the mouth using the end of the decorating tip, and mark the eyes and nose with the small end of the ball tool.

3 For the neck, shape ½ oz (14 g) brown paste into a sausage. Insert dry spaghetti so that they stick out of one end by at least 1 in (2.5 cm). Dab a little edible glue onto this end and push the dry spaghetti through the body to secure the neck in place. Leave to dry.

2 For the body, shape 1 oz (28 g) brown paste into an egg and attach to the legs using edible glue and the dry spaghetti. Support until dry.

1 For the legs, roll 1 oz (28 g) brown paste into a sausage and cut into four. Insert dry spaghetti through each one so that they protrude from both ends. For the hooves, roll four small pinches of brown paste into a ball and attach to the legs using edible glue and the dry spaghetti. Stick the legs together and mold the hooves. Leave to dry.

5 Make the eyes from two pinches of black paste and attach to the head using edible glue.

6 Shape two pinches of brown paste into two triangles for the ears and indent the center with the flattened end of the flower veining tool. Attach to the head using edible glue.

7 Shape two stirrups from the orange paste. Flatten and cut out the center with the X-acto knife. Use the flower veining tool to reshape and neaten them.

8 Add ⅛ oz (4 g) white paste to the remnants of the brown paste (about ½ oz, 14 g) and mix thoroughly. For the strap, pinch off a small amount, roll into a sausage and flatten. Cut a strip approximately 2½ in (6.5 cm) long and ¼ in (6 mm) wide using the pizza cutter. Use the tracing wheel to indent around the edges. Insert one end of the strap through each stirrup, fold the strap back and use edible glue to secure in place. Attach over the horse's back using edible glue.

9 For the saddle, roll the rest of the light brown paste into a ball and flatten the center, leaving a broader edge. Make into a more oval shape. Attach on top of the strap using edible glue.

10 For the mane and tail, add a small amount of shortening to the black paste and blend. Extrude through the clay gun with the multihole disk. Attach the strands to the head and the back of the body with edible glue.

17 piglet

This little piggy went to market, this little piggy stayed at home, and this little piggy would look great on a farmyard-themed cake.

Materials

- Modeling paste
- Corn starch
- Edible glue
- Dry spaghetti

Tools

- Workboard
- Rolling pin
- Flower veining tool
- X-acto knife
- Bone tool

Colors Used

- 3 oz (84 g) pink
- Pinch black

Length: 3½ in (9 cm)

See also
Pastes, icings, glues, pages 28–33 > Designing your figures, pages 48–51 > Props, pages 248–253

4 Mark the eyes with the bone tool. Roll two eyes from the black paste and attach with edible glue.

5 Shape each ear from less than ¹/₂ oz (14 g) of pink paste. Roll into a cone, then flatten with the flat end of the flower veining tool. Attach to the head with edible glue.

3 Indent the front of the nose with the flower veining tool, and use the X-acto knife to cut a mouth.

2 Shape the body from 1½ oz (42 g) pink paste. Roll into a long sausage, with one end fatter than the other. Narrow slightly at the waist area, and narrow again around the nose area, flattening the end for the nose. Place the body on top of the legs, using edible glue and dry spaghetti to secure in place.

1 Shape the hooves from ¾ oz (21 g) pink paste. Shape the back ones slightly larger than the front ones. Roll into a cone, flattening the top and bottom, and use the flower veining tool to indent the front of each hoof. Leave to dry (the hooves need to be fairly dry before you add the body otherwise they will be flattened).

6 Shape the tail from the remnants of pink paste. Roll into a thin cone, coil and twist the top, and attach in place using edible glue.

sheep

He may look goofy but beneath that woolly hair resides a highly intelligent grass-eating machine!

Materials

- Modeling paste
- Corn starch
- Dry spaghetti
- Edible glue

Tools

- Workboard
- Rolling pin
- Flower veining tool
- Texture mat
- Small palette knife

Colors Used

3½ oz (98 g) pink
3½ oz (98 g) white
● Pinch black

Height: 4 in (10 cm)

See also
Pastes, icings, glues, pages 28–33 > Designing your figures, pages 48–51 > Props, pages 248–253

4 Add two ears from ¼ oz (7 g) pink paste, shape into two teardrops, then indent down the center of the teardrop with the flower veining tool. Attach the ears to the head using edible glue.

5 Add a ¼ oz (7 g) white paste to the top of the head, as a furry top patch, securing with edible glue.

3 The head is made from 1 oz (28 g) pink paste. Roll into an egg shape, then flatten the ends slightly. Indent the eye sockets using the pointed end of the flower veining tool. Mark the mouth with the small palette knife, and add two tiny pink dots of paste for the nostrils onto the front of the broad section, indenting them slightly using the pointed end of the flower veining tool. Attach the head to the body using edible glue and dry spaghetti.

6 Finish the sheep by adding two pinches of white paste for eyeballs and two tiny pinches of black paste for pupils, securing both with edible glue.

2 Shape the body from 3 oz (84 g) white paste. Roll into a ball and use the texture mat to form the woolly body. Attach the hooves to the base of the body using dry spaghetti and edible glue.

1 Make four hooves from 2 oz (56 g) pink paste. Roll into four balls, then indent with the flower veining tool to impress the hooves. Leave to dry.

19 turkey

A perfect topper for your Thanksgiving celebration cake.

Materials

- Modeling paste
- Corn starch
- Edible glue
- Dry spaghetti

Tools

- Workboard
- Rolling pin
- Flower veining tool
- X-acto knife
- Pizza cutter

Colors Used

- 3 oz (84 g) chestnut
- 1 oz (28 g) white
- 1 oz (28 g) black
- ½ oz (14 g) light brown
- ¼ oz (7 g) yellow
- ⅛ oz (4 g) red

Height: 2¾ in (7 cm)

See also
Pastes, icings, glues, pages 28–33 > Modeling techniques, pages 42–47 > Designing a cake, pages 52–53

4 Make the hat from 1 oz (28 g) black paste. Take a pinch of paste and roll into a ball. Flatten with the rolling pin and cut out the hat's brim. Use the remaining paste to shape into a cylinder. Pinch the edges to sharpen. Attach the two pieces together, then the hat to the head, with edible glue.

5 Decorate the hat with a white band made from ¼ oz (7 g) white paste. Roll into a sausage, then flatten. Neaten with the pizza cutter and attach the band around the hat with edible glue. To make the buckle, roll ⅛ oz (4 g) yellow paste into a ball, flatten, and cut out a square using the X-acto knife. Cut the inside of the square out, leaving a buckle shape. Attach as before.

3 Attach two pinches of white paste, then two black pupils to the head with edible glue to create the eyes.

6 Make a beak from ⅛ oz (4 g) yellow paste shaped into a triangle and bent down slightly. Attach to the face using edible glue. Make the wattle from the red paste. Shape into a tapered teardrop. Attach around the beak with edible glue.

2 For the tail, roll ½ oz (14 g) each of chestnut, light brown and white paste for the sausages. Attach together with edible glue. Curl around into a semicircle, filling the center with a flattened ball of about ¼ oz (7 g) white paste. Flatten together and score down the tail with the flower veining tool. Use the X-acto knife to cut out sections of the white paste that correspond with the scored lines. Attach to the body using edible glue and dry spaghetti.

1 Make the body from 2 oz (56 g) chestnut paste. Shape into a ball, then pull the top slightly, narrow the neck of this so you have a head and neck. Score the body lightly using the flower veining tool to represent feathers.

7 Make the wings from ½ oz (14 g) chestnut paste. Roll into two teardrops, then score the paste with the flower veining tool from the broad end to the narrow end. Attach with edible glue.

20 bat

Tweak this cute bat's fangs and you'll create a much scarier version.

Materials

- Modeling paste
- Gum paste
- Corn starch
- Edible glue

Tools

- Workboard
- Rolling pin
- Decorating tip No. 1
- Flower veining tool
- X-acto knife

Colors Used

- ● 2¼ oz (63 g) black modeling paste
- ● 2 oz (56 g) black gum paste
- ○ ⅛ oz (4 g) white

Length: 2 in (5 cm)

See also
Pastes, icings, glues, pages 28–33 > Modeling techniques, pages 42–47 > Designing your figures, pages 48–51

3 Shape the eyes from the white paste (pinch off a tiny bit for the two teeth). Shape the remaining into two teardrops. Flatten slightly and attach to the body with edible glue. Add two tiny black pupils from a pinch of remnant paste using edible glue to secure in place.

4 For the eyebrows, thinly roll out a pinch of black gum paste. Using the end of a small decorating tip, cut out a small disk, then adjust the decorating tip to cut off two edges of the circle for the eyebrows. Attach to the eyes using edible glue.

5 Shape the two ears from the remaining ¼ oz (7 g) black paste. Roll into a teardrop, and flatten the center using the flat end of the flower veining tool. Leave the outer edge of the ears unflattened. Shape into a rough triangle and attach to the body using edible glue.

2 Cut the wings from 2 oz (56 g) black gum paste using the X-acto knife. Lay flat and mark the lines on the wings using the flat end of the flower veining tool. Leave to dry. When dry, insert into the slits made in the body. Secure in place with a little softened remnant of black gum paste and edible glue.

1 Shape the body from 2 oz (56 g) black modeling paste. Mark the mouth using the end of a decorating tip or use the flower veining tool. Cut two slits either side slightly toward the back of the ball shape. These are to insert the wings into when they're dry.

6 Shape the teeth from the remaining pinch of white paste, shaping two tiny triangles. Attach with edible glue.

otter

Subtle texturing of the muzzle and fur really bring this otter to life.

Materials

- Modeling paste
- Corn starch
- Edible glue
- Dry spaghetti

Tools

- Workboard
- Rolling pin
- Bone tool
- Flower veining tool

Colors Used

- 2½ oz (70 g) brown
- ¼ oz (7 g) light brown
- Pinch black

Length: 3½ in (9 cm)

See also

Pastes, icings, glues, pages 28–33 > Modeling techniques, pages 42–47 > Designing your figures, pages 48–51

8 For the furry tummy, roll the light brown paste out thinly into an oval. Slice the oval vertically to create a flat end, and score the paste using the pointed end of the flower veining tool. Attach the "fur" to the front of the body, tucking the straight end under the chin. Secure with edible glue.

7 The ears are shaped from two tiny balls of brown paste. Flatten the center using the small end of the bone tool. Secure to the head using edible glue.

6 Make the nose and eyes from a pinch of black paste. Roll into three balls, one larger than the other two, and attach to the face using edible glue.

5. For the muzzle, roll two pinches of brown paste into two balls and secure to the face using edible glue. Indent the muzzle with the pointed end of the flower veining tool. Add a pinch of paste, shaped into a tiny sausage, underneath the muzzle for the mouth.

4 For the forelegs, mold ⅛ oz (4 g) brown paste into two sausage shapes and indent using the pointed end of the flower veining tool to shape the paws. Attach to the body using edible glue.

1 Shape the body from 1 oz (28 g) brown paste. Mold into a long sausage, thinning one end for the tail. Coil the tail around, but bend up the opposite end to create a body.

2 Shape the two rear legs from ½ oz (14 g) brown paste. Split into two teardrops, flatten, and work the narrower end into the back foot. Flatten up against the tail, securing in place using edible glue.

3 For the head, shape ½ oz (14 g) brown paste into a soft cone shape and indent the eye sockets with the small end of the bone tool. Attach to the body using edible glue and dry spaghetti.

22 squirrel

This deep chestnut squirrel is characterized by his big bushy tail.

Materials

- Modeling paste
- Corn starch
- Edible glue
- Dry spaghetti

Tools

- Workboard
- Rolling pin
- Ball tool
- Flower veining tool
- X-acto knife

Colors Used

- 6½ oz (182 g) chestnut
- ¾ oz (21 g) white
- Pinch black
- Pinch pink
- Pinch cream

Height: 4 in (10 cm)

See also
Pastes, icings, glues, pages 28–33 > Modeling techniques, pages 42–47 > Props, pages 248–253

4 Create a pyramid out of pink paste for the nose and attach to the face with edible glue.

3 Shape the ears from two tiny pinches of chestnut paste. Roll each into a ball, flatten, and soften using the ball tool. Pinch the base and cut off a little to flatten the end. Attach the flat end to the head with edible glue.

5 Make the cheeks from ½ oz (14 g) white paste. Roll into two balls and attach just below the nose with edible glue. Prick with the end of the flower veining tool. Roll out a pinch of white paste and cut teeth using the X-acto knife. Attach to the bottom of the cheeks with edible glue.

2 For the head, shape 1 oz (28 g) chestnut paste into a small cone, marking the eye sockets with the smaller end of the ball tool. Attach to the body using edible glue and dry spaghetti. Roll two tiny black balls of paste for the eyes and attach with edible glue.

6 For the tummy, blend a pinch of white paste with a pinch of chestnut paste. Roll the mixed paste thinly and cut out a circle. Attach to the body using edible glue.

1 Roll and shape 2 oz (56 g) chestnut paste into a fat cone for the body.

7 For the front paws, roll ½ oz (14 g) chestnut paste into two sausages. Narrow in the middle and, using the flower veining tool, indent the paws. Attach to the body using edible glue.

10 Make the tail from 2 oz (56 g) chestnut paste. Roll into a long banana shape, coil one end, and tuck the other under the squirrel's body. Secure with edible glue. Support until dry.

9 For the back paws, roll 1 oz (28 g) chestnut paste into two teardrops, flatten, and indent the broader end using the flower veining tool. Push the narrower end under the body and secure with edible glue.

8 Make a nut from the cream paste. Roll into an almond shape and attach to the front paws with edible glue.

23 chipmunk

Watch this cheeky chipmunk doesn't steal any of your paste.

Materials

- Modeling paste
- Corn starch
- Edible glue
- Light, mid- and dark brown petal dusts

Tools

- Workboard
- Rolling pin
- Small palette knife
- X-acto knife
- Flower veining tool
- Dusting brush

Colors Used

- 5¾ oz (161 g) cream
- Pinch black

Length: 3½ in (9 cm)

See also
Pastes, icings, glues, pages 28–33 > Color mixing, pages 38–39 > Modeling techniques, pages 42–47

5 Roll a pinch of black paste into a triangle and attach to the face with edible glue for the nose. Use ¼ oz (7 g) cream paste rolled into two balls for the muzzle. Flatten and attach using edible glue. Prick with the pointed end of the flower veining tool to texture.

4 Make the head from 1 oz (28 g) cream paste, shaped into an elongated oval. Shape two cheek pouches from ½ oz (14 g) cream paste. Roll into two semicircles and attach to the face using edible glue. Use the flat end of the flower veining tool to smooth the join between the cheek and face.

6 Shape ½ oz (14 g) cream paste into a ball for the ears. Cut in half and soften the center, thinning a little. Attach to the head using edible glue. Add two eyes from a pinch of black paste.

3 Shape the front legs from ½ oz (14 g) cream paste. Roll into two long sausages, thinner at one end for the paws. Cut four fingers using the X-acto knife. Attach the paws to the front of the body using edible glue.

2 Roll two short sausage shapes from ½ oz (14 g) cream paste for the back feet, flatten, and use the X-acto knife to cut four long, tapered toes. Attach beneath the back leg indentations using edible glue.

7 Roll 1 oz (28 g) cream paste into a banana shape and flatten one end for the tail. Tuck the flat end under the body using edible glue to secure.

1 For the body, shape 1½ oz (42 g) cream paste into an oval and flatten one end, ready for the head. Indent either side of the back of the body using the small palette knife to shape the back legs.

8 Dust the chipmunk in stripes using light, mid- and dark brown petal dusts.

24 deer

Turn this deer into Rudolf for a Christmas-themed cake by giving him a red nose.

Materials

- Modeling paste
- Corn starch
- Dry spaghetti
- Edible glue
- 26 ga. florist's wire
- Florist's tape
- Brown edible paint

Tools

- Workboard
- Rolling pin
- Small palette knife
- Flower veining tool
- X-acto knife
- Paint brush

Colors Used

- 3½ oz (98 g) brown
- ¾ oz (21 g) cream
- Pinch black

Height: 4½ in (11 cm)

See also

Pastes, icings, glues, pages 28–33 > Modeling techniques, pages 42–47 > Designing your figures, pages 48–51

4 Shape the ears from two pinches of brown paste. Roll into a teardrop, then score down the center with the pointed end of the flower veining tool. Trim the fatter end with the X-acto knife and attach to the head using edible glue.

5 Shape the antlers from the 26 ga. florist's wire. Cut into five equal pieces and attach together at the base with florist's tape. Leaving the central wire straight, bend two wires off at ¼ in (6 mm) and again at ¾ in (1.8 cm). Trim, then paint the wires using brown edible paint. Push the base of the antlers into the head.

3 Shape the head from 1 oz (28 g) brown paste. Roll into a teardrop, flatten the top, and mark the mouth using the small palette knife. Attach to the body using edible glue and dry spaghetti. Attach two tiny black eyes and a black nose, made from pinches of black paste.

2 Shape 1½ oz (42 g) brown paste into an elongated oval for the body. Attach the legs using dots of edible glue. Support it standing until dry.

6 Use ¼ oz (7 g) cream paste to make the furry chest. Shape into a teardrop and texture using the flower veining tool. Attach with edible glue. Finish the deer by adding little cream dots to its back.

1 Roll 1 oz (28 g) brown paste into four thin legs. Insert dry spaghetti down each leg. Leave a little sticking out at the top, then re-roll to smooth out the shape. Indent hooves with the small palette knife. Leave to dry.

25 fox

This playful fox adds a touch of bright color to your cake.

Materials

- Modeling paste
- Corn starch
- Dry spaghetti
- Edible glue
- Royal icing

Tools

- Workboard
- Rolling pin
- Small palette knife
- Flower veining tool
- Ball tool
- Paint brush

Colors Used

- 4 oz (112 g) orange
- ½ oz (14 g) white
- Pinch black

Height: 3½ in (9 cm)

See also
Pastes, icings, glues, pages 28–33 > Color mixing, pages 38–39 > Modeling techniques, pages 42–47

3 Shape the head from 1 oz (28 g) orange paste. Shape into a cone, broadening and thinning either side of the base. Texture the thinning area with the pointed end of the flower veining tool. Indent the eye sockets with the ball tool and indent the mouth with the small palette knife.

4 Shape the ears from ½ oz (14 g) orange paste. Shape two triangles, flattening the center of each with the flower veining tool. Attach to the head with edible glue.

5 Add two eyes to the head made from pinches of black paste. Shape the nose from a pinch of black paste. Shape into a triangle and attach to the snout.

2 Make the furry chest from ½ oz (14 g) white paste. Shape into a teardrop, flatten, and use the flower veining tool to texture. Attach to the chest of the fox with edible glue.

6 Shape the forelegs from ½ oz (14 g) orange paste. Roll into two teardrops, wrap the narrow end around the back of the fox, and indent the paws with the end of the flower veining tool.

1 Shape the body from 1 oz (28 g) orange paste. Roll into a cone, making the base broader and the neck a little narrower. Insert dry spaghetti in the neck for the head. Indent either side of the broad section with the small palette knife, marking the outline of the back legs.

7 Make the rear feet from ¼ oz (7 g) orange paste. Shape into tiny teardrops, indenting the paws as before. Secure in place with edible glue.

9 Paint the face and tip of the tail with the royal icing. Draw the flower veining tool through the royal icing after a minute or two to give a textured effect.

8 For the tail, shape ¾ oz (21 g) orange paste into a banana with tapered ends. Tuck one end under the body, securing with edible glue, and bend the other end round, securing the body of the tail to the back of the fox.

moose

This moose is rather proud of his magnificent antlers.

Materials

- Modeling paste
- Corn starch
- Edible glue
- Dry spaghetti
- Pink petal dust
- Brown petal dust

Tools

- Workboard
- Rolling pin
- Small palette knife
- Ball tool
- Flower veining tool
- X-acto knife
- Dusting brush

Colors Used

- 5 oz (140 g) dark brown
  1 oz (28 g) cream
- Pinch black

Height: 4½ in (11 cm)

See also
Pastes, icings, glues, pages 28–33 > Modeling techniques, pages 42–47 > Designing your figures, pages 48–51

5 For the antlers, roll 1 oz (28 g) cream paste into two teardrops and flatten. Using the X-acto knife, cut out triangular shapes from the outer edge of each antler. Attach to the head using dry spaghetti. Push the strand into the antler, then into the head.

4 Make the ears from ½ oz (14 g) brown paste. Roll into two teardrops and draw the pointed end of the flower veining tool down the ear. Attach to the head using edible glue.

6 Dust the cheeks with a little pink petal dust. Dust the antlers with a little brown petal dust.

3 For the head, roll 1 oz (28 g) brown paste into a cone. Add two tiny brown balls for the nostrils, and indent the center with the small end of the ball tool. Mark the mouth with the small palette knife. Indent each end of the mouth with the small end of the ball tool. Add two tiny black dots for eyes. Secure to the body using edible glue and insert onto the dry spaghetti.

2 Make the body from 2 oz (56 g) brown paste. Roll into an oval shape and attach to the feet with edible glue. Push dry spaghetti through the front of the body in preparation for the head.

1 Shape the feet from 1½ oz (42 g) brown paste. Roll into four cones and indent the hooves with the small palette knife. Stick the feet together and put dry spaghetti through each one. Leave to dry.

27 bear

Change the color of the lollipop to suit the design scheme of your cake.

Materials

- Modeling paste
- Corn starch
- Edible glue
- Lollipop stick
- Dry spaghetti

Tools

- Workboard
- Rolling pin
- Flower veining tool
- Tracing tool
- Ball tool
- X-acto knife

Colors Used

- 5½ oz (154 g) brown
- ½ oz (14 g) cream
- ¼ oz (7 g) white
- ¼ oz (7 g) red
- Pinch black
- Pinch pink

Height: 3½ in (9 cm)

See also
Pastes, icings, glues, pages 28–33 > Modeling techniques, pages 42–47 > Props, pages 248–253

4 Shape 1 oz (28 g) brown paste into a pear for the head, flattening the front as you did for the body; this will accentuate the muzzle. Run the tracing wheel up the front of the face. Attach to the body using edible glue and dry spaghetti. Roll two pinches of black paste into balls for the eyes. Secure on the face with edible glue.

3 Roll 1 oz (28 g) brown paste into two elongated teardrops for the front paws. Use the flower veining tool to indent the paws and the tracing wheel to texture. Attach to the top of the body with edible glue. Position one paw out sideways next to the body. Put a lollipop stick into the paw of the other, ready for the lollipop. Secure with edible glue.

5 Make the ears from the remaining brown paste. Roll into two balls, flatten, indent with the ball tool, and trim off a little with the X-acto knife to give a flat side. Secure the flat side to the head. Run the tracing wheel over the ears.

6 Roll the cream paste into a ball for the muzzle, flatten slightly, and indent the sides with the flower veining tool. Create a mouth using the small end of the ball tool. Shape a tiny pinch of black paste into a pyramid for the nose and attach to the top of the muzzle with edible glue. Shape a pinch of pink paste for the tongue, and attach with edible glue.

7 Make the lollipop from two sausages of paste, one white, one red. Stick together, then twist. Roll up, securing with edible glue as you go. Cut off any excess, then push onto the lollipop stick. Secure with edible glue.

2 For the lower legs split 1 oz (28 g) brown paste into two sausages, narrowing one end. Tuck the narrow end under the body and secure with edible glue. Indent the paws with the flower veining tool, then run the tracing tool along the edge.

1 Shape the body from 2 oz (56 g) brown paste. Mold into a pear shape, flattening the tummy with the flat section of the flower veining tool. Run the tracing tool up the tummy of the bear to indent the paste.

28 porcupine

Make the spikes of your porcupine as long as you like.

Materials

- Modeling paste
- Corn starch
- Edible glue
- Dry spaghetti

Tools

- Workboard
- Rolling pin
- Flower veining tool
- Ball tool
- Decorating tip No. 1

Colors Used

- ⬤ 3½ oz (98 g) brown
- ⬤ ¼ oz (7 g) white
- ⬤ Pinch black

Length: 2¾ in (7 cm)

See also
Pastes, icings, glues, pages 28–33 > Color mixing, pages 38–39 > Modeling techniques, pages 42–47

2 Shape the body from 2 oz (56 g) brown paste. Mold into an oval, elongate one end slightly to give a little snout, and mark the eye sockets using the ball tool. Mark the mouth using the end of the decorating tip. Attach the body to the legs using dry spaghetti and dabs of edible glue.

3 Use two tiny pinches of black paste rolled into balls for the eyes. Attach with edible glue. Roll the remaining black paste into a ball for the nose and attach with edible glue.

1 Make the paws from 1 oz (28 g) brown paste. Roll into four equal balls, flatten slightly, and use the sharp end of the flower veining tool to mark the paws. Stick all four feet together. Leave to dry.

4 Make the spines by roughly blending the white paste with the remaining brown paste. Roll pinches of the paste in the palm of your hand, leaving one end broad and the other pointed. Attach to the back of the porcupine using edible glue. Start at the back of the body and work forward.

29 raccoon

The striped tail of this cute raccoon is very eye-catching.

Materials	Tools
• Modeling paste	• Workboard
• Corn starch	• Rolling pin
• Dry spaghetti	• X-acto knife
• Edible glue	• Paper towel
	• Flower veining tool
	• Pizza cutter

Colors Used

⬤ 3½ oz (98 g) gray
⬤ 1 oz (28 g) white
⬤ ½ oz (14 g) black

Height: 5 in (13 cm)

See also
Pastes, icings, glues, pages 28–33 > Modeling techniques, pages 42–47 > Designing your figures, pages 48–51

5 For the whiskers, roll out ¼ oz (7 g) white paste and cut a triangle using the X-acto knife. Trim off the top point. Cut a slit out of the top and curve the shape either side. Cut three further whiskers, then use the flower veining tool to add texture. Attach to the face using edible glue and dry spaghetti.

4 For the head, shape ½ oz (14 g) gray paste into a softened cone. Flatten the eye section slightly using the flat end of the flower veining tool. Bulge out the muzzle. Attach to the body using edible glue and dry spaghetti.

3 For the chest, shape ½ oz (14 g) white paste into a long, thin cone and flatten. Use the flower veining tool to texture by drawing the tool down the cone. Secure to the body between the arms using edible glue.

2 For the arms, roll ½ oz (14 g) gray paste into two sausages, but thin one end slightly for the hand. Use the X-acto knife to mark the fingers. Attach to the body using edible glue, one across the front and one across the back, to give the sideways look. Support with paper towel until firm.

1 For the body, shape 1 oz (28 g) gray paste into a tall cone and push dry spaghetti through the top to support the head.

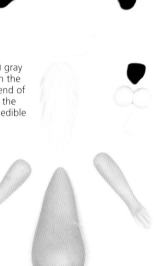

11 Make two feet from pinches of black paste and attach under the front of the body.

6 For the eye patches, cut two kidney shapes from a pinch of black paste using the X-acto knife. Attach to the whisker section with edible glue, curving round to complement the shape you have cut. Add two tiny balls of black paste for the eyes.

7 For the muzzle, shape two pinches of white paste into balls. Attach to the face with edible glue, pushing them together. Add a tiny dot of black paste for the nose. Roll a tiny pinch of white paste into a sausage and attach underneath the muzzle for the mouth using edible glue.

8 For the ears, shape two pinches of gray paste into tiny teardrops and flatten using the pointed end of the flower veining tool. Cut off the point and attach to the head using edible glue.

9 Make three tufts of hair by rolling tiny pinches of gray paste in the palm of your hand. Attach with edible glue.

10 For the tail, roll 1 oz (28 g) gray paste into a teardrop, but elongate the fat end slightly to secure to the underside of the body. Attach the tail up the back of the body. Roll out the remaining black paste. Use the pizza cutter to cut strips of paste. Attach them around the tail using edible glue.

30 beaver

This cheeky beaver has a rather mischievous expression on his face.

Materials
- Modeling paste
- Corn starch
- Edible glue
- Dry spaghetti
- Edible white paint

Tools
- Workboard
- Rolling pin
- Flower veining tool
- Ball tool
- Paint brush

Colors Used
- 3 oz (84 g) medium brown
- ¾ oz (21 g) white
- ½ oz (14 g) dark brown
- ⅛ oz (4 g) light brown
- Pinch black

Height: 4½ in (11 cm)

See also
Pastes, icings, glues, pages 28–33 > Modeling techniques, pages 42–47 > Designing your figures, pages 48–51

3 Shape ½ oz (14 g) medium-brown paste into a rough triangle for the head. Indent the eye sockets with the small end of the ball tool. Attach to the body using edible glue and dry spaghetti if desired.

4 For the ears, roll two tiny pinches of medium-brown paste into two balls, flatten with the small end of the ball tool, and attach to the head using edible glue.

5 Shape the eyes in the usual way, using tiny dots of white paste topped with black. Finish by painting a white dot on the black of the eyes, using edible white paint. Secure the eyes in the eye sockets using edible glue.

2 Make the arms from ½ oz (14 g) medium-brown paste. Shape into two short sausages. Narrow one end slightly for the hand and narrow a little further at the wrist section. Attach to the body at shoulder level, wrapping the arm around the body and securing in place with edible glue. Indent the hands with the flower veining tool to represent fingers.

6 Shape the muzzle from ½ oz (14 g) white paste. Roll into two equal balls, flatten on the base, and attach to the face using edible glue. Prick with the pointed end of the flower veining tool. Attach a black nose, shaped from a pinch of black paste, using edible glue.

1 Shape the body from 1 oz (28 g) medium-brown paste. Roll into an egg shape, and sit up on the broad end. Use the pointed end of the flower veining tool to mark lines for the back legs. Flatten the light brown paste and shape into an oval. Cut off one curved end, then attach to the chest using edible glue.

7 Make the teeth from the remaining white paste. Roll out the paste and cut a rectangle, marking a line down the center to form two front teeth. Secure in place using edible glue.

9 Shape the feet from the remaining medium brown modeling paste. Roll two teardrop shapes, flatten and mark the toes of the beaver. Attach to the base of the body using edible glue.

8 Make the tail from the dark brown modeling paste. Roll into a rough oval shape. Flatten and score the top with the flower veining tool. Attach to the base of the beaver using edible glue.

3 | owl

You can make the owl in different shades of brown or any other color you choose.

Materials	Tools
• Modeling paste	• Workboard
• Corn starch	• Rolling pin
• Dry spaghetti	• Heart cutter
• Edible glue	• Flower veining tool
• Dark pink petal	• Ball tool
dust	• Dusting brush

Colors Used

5 oz (140 g) pink
1¼ oz (35 g) white

Height: 3½ in (9 cm)

See also
Pastes, icings, glues, pages 28–33 > Color mixing, pages 38–39 > Modeling techniques, pages 42–47

4 Shape ¼ oz (7 g) white paste into two long, thin, tapered sausage shapes and add these to the head to further accentuate the ridge.

5 Take three different pinches of pink paste, roll into three different-sized teardrops, and attach to the top of the head.

3 Make the head from 2 oz (56 g) pink paste. Shape into a flattened cylinder and accentuate the top edge, softening the paste under the edge, curving it in, while sharpening the top edge. Draw a section of the ridge forward for the face. Use the pointed end of the flower veining tool to accentuate this.

6 Make the eyes by rolling two pinches of pink paste into a ball. Flatten the balls, and texture the paste with the flower veining tool. Cut off a little arc so that the eye fits neatly up against the nose and attach to the head. Indent the center of the eye with the small end of the ball tool. Roll two pinches of pink paste into balls, attach these to the eyes, and add a smaller, flat, pale pink ball. Finish the eyes with a tiny ball of white paste on top. Attach all components using edible glue.

2 Using the cutter, cut out a heart shape from ½ oz (14 g) rolled-out white paste. Attach to the chest using edible glue.

1 Shape the body into a cone using 2 oz (56 g) pink paste. Soften the top and push dry spaghetti through the neck section to support the head.

7 Make the nose from ⅛ oz (4 g) white paste shaped into a fat triangle. Attach with edible glue.

10 Finish by dusting with a dark pink petal dust.

8 Shape two wings from ½ oz (14 g) pink paste. Shape into two ovals. Flatten using the rolling pin, then score the wings using the flower veining tool. Draw lines down the wings from one end, allowing the tool to run off the end. Attach to the body using edible glue.

9 Make the feet from ½ oz (7 g) white paste. Shape into two teardrops, flatten, and use the flower veining tool to mark the claws. Draw the tool from the broad end to the narrow end twice on each foot. Attach to the underside of the body using edible glue.

blue tit

A very colorful British garden bird for your avian-themed cake.

Materials

- Modeling paste
- Corn starch
- Edible glue
- Edible black paint
- Dry spaghetti

Tools

- Workboard
- Rolling pin
- Flower veining tool
- X-acto knife
- Fine paint brush

Colors Used

- 2½ oz (70 g) pale blue
- 1 oz (28 g) yellow
- ⅝ oz (18 g) white
- ½ oz (14 g) black
- ¼ oz (7 g) green

Length: 2 in (5 cm)

See also
Pastes, icings, glues, pages 28–33 > Modeling techniques, pages 42–47 > Props, pages 248–253

3 Roll out 1 oz (28 g) blue paste and shape into two teardrops for the wings. Texture with the flower veining tool. Cut thinly rolled green paste into two squares using the X-acto knife, and secure in place on the wing using edible glue. Add a thin strip of black and white to the wing along the lower green edge, securing in place with edible glue. Attach the wing to the body in the same way.

4 Shape a beak from a pinch of black paste, rolled into a pointed cone, and attach with edible glue. Make eyes from two pinches of black paste and secure as before. Paint stripes on the face of the bird with a fine paint brush and edible black paint.

2 Roll out ¼ oz (7 g) black paste. Make a round disk shape and attach to the neck section with edible glue.

5 For the head, roll the white paste into a ball and attach to the body using dry spaghetti and edible glue.

1 Shape the yellow paste into a tapered teardrop for the body. Texture with the flower veining tool to give the impression of feathers.

7 Roll out the remaining pale blue paste and cut out a triangle shape with the X-acto knife. Texture with the flower veining tool and attach to the tail end using edible glue.

6 Use ⅛ oz (4 g) pale blue paste for the hair. Roll into a rough circle, texture with the flower veining tool, and attach to the head of the bird with edible glue.

33 chick

This chick is made from white modeling chocolate colored with petal dust. However, it could easily be made from modeling paste or marzipan.

Materials

- Modeling paste
- Chocolate modeling paste
- Corn starch
- Orange petal dust
- Dark orange petal dust
- Edible glue
- Edible white paint

Tools

- Workboard
- Rolling pin
- Plastic bag
- Sheets of plastic
- X-acto knife
- Paint brush
- Flower veining tool

Colors Used

- 4 oz (112 g) orange modeling chocolate
- ½ oz (14 g) white modeling chocolate
- ½ oz (14 g) dark orange modeling chocolate
- ½ oz (14 g) white
- Pinch black

Height: 2¾ in (7 cm)

See also
Pastes, icings, glues, pages 28–33 > Modeling techniques, pages 42–47 > Designing your figures, pages 48–51

3 Shape the white modeling chocolate into a rough oval. Flatten between two sheets of plastic. This keeps the fingermarks off the paste as well as reducing the chances that your fingers will start melting the chocolate. Trim to a neat oval using the X-acto knife and attach to the chest using edible glue.

4 For the head, roll 1 oz (28 g) orange modeling chocolate into a ball and attach to the body.

2 Roll 2 oz (56 g) orange modeling chocolate into a ball for the body.

1 Color 4 oz (112 g) white modeling chocolate with orange petal dust and ½ oz (14 g) with dark orange petal dust. Blend thoroughly and work quickly. Leave the paste for a few hours in a plastic bag to cool down.

5 Make the eyes from the white modeling paste. Shape one large and one small ball. Flatten slightly and attach to the head with edible glue. Add two black pupils using the black paste. Add a tiny white dot on each eye with edible white paint. Add two eyebrows using a pinch of orange modeling chocolate. Shape into elongated ovals and attach above the eyes. Use the flower veining tool to texture slightly. Add a beak using a pinch of orange modeling chocolate, shape into a triangle, and attach to the face with edible glue.

7 Shape the feet from the dark orange modeling chocolate. Roll into two teardrops, and use the flower veining tool to indent the feet. Attach with edible glue.

6 Make the wings from the remaining orange modeling chocolate. Flatten two ovals between plastic sheets, thinning at the edges. Attach to the sides of the body using edible glue.

eagle

Is this a benevolent eagle or has he got his eyes on something for lunch?

Materials

- Modeling paste
- Corn starch
- Edible glue
- Dry spaghetti

Tools

- Workboard
- Rolling pin
- X-acto knife
- Flower veining tool
- Scallop tool

Colors Used

- 3 oz (84 g) brown
- 2¾ oz (77 g) white
- 2½ oz (70 g) yellow
- Pinch black

Height: 3½ in (9 cm)

See also
Pastes, icings, glues, pages 28–33 > Modeling techniques, pages 42–47 > Designing your figures, pages 48–51

4 For the beak, roll the remaining yellow paste into a cone, trim off the base end to sharpen the edges, and curve the pointed end over slightly. Use the flower veining tool to mark the upper and lower beak section and attach to the head with dry spaghetti.

5 Shape a pinch of white paste into two teardrops and attach to the head using edible glue. Add two pinches of black paste on top to create eyes.

6 Shape 1 oz (28 g) brown paste into two teardrops. Using the scallop tool, indent the long side of each teardrop to give a feathered effect. Mark more feathers on each of the wings. Attach to the back using edible glue.

3 Shape 2 oz (56 g) white paste into a fat sausage shape for the head. Pinch one end to sharpen the edges and, at the same time, bevel the center so it fits neatly with the body. Use the X-acto knife to cut triangles out of the sharpened edge, to give a feathered appearance. Use the flower veining tool to texture the neck section and give the impression of feathers. Attach to the body using edible glue and dry spaghetti.

2 Make the claws from ½ oz (14 g) yellow paste. Roll into two teardrops, flatten using the X-acto knife, and cut out two triangles from the broad end. Attach to the underside of the body using edible glue. Use the flower veining tool to score down the front of the body to create two legs.

1 Shape 2 oz (56 g) brown paste into a teardrop. Bend the fatter end around to create the body.

7 Make the tail feathers from ½ oz (14 g) white paste. Shape into a teardrop, then flatten. Score the tail with the flower veining tool to create a feathered effect. Indent the edge. Attach using edible glue.

35 flamingo

The flamingo is not an easy bird to make with its long legs and long neck, but with a little practice, you will create some great-looking results.

Materials

- Modeling paste
- Corn starch
- Edible glue
- One 3-in (7.5-cm) and two 6-in (15-cm) lengths 22 ga. pink wire
- Two flower spikes

Tools

- Workboard
- Rolling pin
- Flower veining tool
- Wire cutters

Colors Used

- 2 oz (56 g) pink
- ¼ oz (7 g) black

Height: 5½ in (14 cm)

See also
Pastes, icings, glues, pages 28–33 > Modeling techniques, pages 42–47 > Props, pages 248–253

4 Shape ⅛ oz (4 g) black paste into a small sausage shape for the beak. Bend in the middle, then attach to the head. Set aside until the end of step 5.

3 Roll ½ oz (14 g) pink paste into a sausage for the neck. Twist and bend a 3-in (7.5-cm) length of 22 ga. wire and thread the sausage down the wire, following the twists and turns. Shape so it is smooth with a bulbous ball shape at the very end (this is the head). Leave a little wire protruding from the opposite end to insert into the body.

5 Decide where you are going to place the bird on your cake. Insert two flower spikes into the cake and fill with the same paste as covers your cake. Insert two 6-in (15-cm) wires into the flower spikes (do not insert wire directly into the cake). Push to the end of the flower spikes and cut the wire once you have about 2 in (5 cm) sticking out from the cake. Insert the body onto the legs, using edible glue to assist. Support the body in position until set. Insert the exposed wire at the base of the neck into the body, allowing the beak to rest on the cake surface.

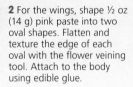

6 Add an eye to the head, using a pinch of black paste, and secure in place with edible glue.

2 For the wings, shape ½ oz (14 g) pink paste into two oval shapes. Flatten and texture the edge of each oval with the flower veining tool. Attach to the body using edible glue.

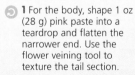

1 For the body, shape 1 oz (28 g) pink paste into a teardrop and flatten the narrower end. Use the flower veining tool to texture the tail section.

baby birds

Delightful baby birds that are cute in any color and any size.

Materials
- Modeling paste
- Corn starch
- Edible glue
- Dry spaghetti
- Colored petal dust

Tools
- Workboard
- Rolling pin
- Paper towel
- Flower veining tool
- X-acto knife
- Dusting brush

Colors Used
1 oz (28 g) colored paste
● Pinch black
● Pinch gold

Length: 1½ in (4 cm)

See also
Pastes, icings, glues, pages 28–33 > Color mixing, pages 38–39 > Modeling techniques, pages 42–47

4 Make the head from a pinch of paste. Roll into a ball and attach to the body with edible glue and dry spaghetti. Add two eyes using a pinch of black paste. Make a beak from the gold paste. Roll a teardrop and then slit the narrow end with the X-acto knife. Attach to the head with edible glue. Position the beak as open as you want.

5 Dust the bird with an appropriately colored petal dust to accentuate the shape and add depth to the model.

3 Make the wings from two large pinches of paste. Shape into a teardrop and flatten slightly. Use the flower veining tool to score the wings to give the impression of feathers. Attach to the body using edible glue and curl the wings outward slightly.

1 Shape the body from ¼ oz (7 g) colored paste of your choice. Shape into a teardrop, allowing the pointed end to form part of the tail. Raise the tail section slightly and support using paper towel.

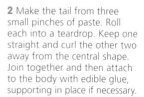

2 Make the tail from three small pinches of paste. Roll each into a teardrop. Keep one straight and curl the other two away from the central shape. Join together and then attach to the body with edible glue, supporting in place if necessary.

37 kingfisher

A majestic bird suitable for a cake fit for a king.

Materials

- Modeling paste
- Corn starch
- Edible glue
- Dry spaghetti
- Edible white paint

Tools

- Workboard
- Rolling pin
- X-acto knife
- Flower veining tool
- Small palette knife
- Fine paint brush

Colors Used

- 2½ oz (70 g) orange
- 2¼ oz (63 g) blue
- 1⅛ oz (32 g) white
- ¾ oz (21 g) black

Height: 3½ in (9 cm)

See also
Pastes, icings, glues, pages 28–33 > Modeling techniques, pages 42–47 > Designing your figures, pages 48–51

6 Roll out three blue head feathers: one broad for the top of the head and two narrow for either side of the face. Use ½ oz (14 g) for the broad feather and ¼ oz (7 g) for the narrow feathers. Roll the paste into teardrops. Place the point of the large teardrop over the forehead, just above where the beak will fit. Attach the others along either cheek.

7 Take two pinches of white paste, flatten, and texture with the flower veining tool. Attach at the end of each blue cheek with edible glue.

8 Fill in between the blue head feathers with ¼ oz (7 g) orange paste. Shape into two elongated ovals, texture with the flower veining tool, and secure to the face with edible glue.

9 Add two black eyes using two pinches of black paste. Secure in place as usual. Add a tiny dot of edible white paint to each eye.

10 For the beak, shape ½ oz (14 g) black paste into a long, pointed cone. Thread dry spaghetti through it for support and attach to the front of the face with edible glue and more dry spaghetti.

5 Shape the head from 1 oz (28 g) white paste. Roll into a ball and attach to the body using edible glue and dry spaghetti.

4 For the wings, shape ½ oz (14 g) blue paste into two teardrops. Flatten and neaten the edges with the small palette knife. Texture the wings using the flower veining tool. Attach wings to the side of the kingfisher.

1 For the body, shape 2 oz (56 g) orange paste into a teardrop. Bend the narrow end over slightly for the tail and use this to stand the body up, with the broader end being the chest section.

3 Roll ¼ oz (7 g) orange paste into two teardrops, flatten, and cut two triangles out of the broad end. This will create three claws. Attach under the front of the body with edible glue.

2 Shape the tail from 1 oz (28 g) blue modeling paste. Roll out thickly into an oval shape and cut off one end. On the curved end, cut out three triangle shapes using the X-acto knife. Curve the corners off to leave a scalloped edge. Draw the flower veining tool up from each scallop to create four feather shapes. Texture the feathers lightly with the flower veining tool. Attach to the tail of the bird using edible glue.

38 duck

The duck is formed from lots of different-colored shapes layered on top of each other.

Materials

- Modeling paste
- Corn starch
- Edible glue
- Dry spaghetti
- Royal icing

Tools

- Workboard
- Rolling pin
- Flower veining tool
- Small palette knife

Colors Used

- 2½ oz (70 g) dark brown
- 1 oz (28 g) white
- 1 oz (28 g) green
- ½ oz (14 g) orange
- ½ oz (14 g) cream
- ½ oz (14 g) black
- ¼ oz (7 g) peach
- ¼ oz (7 g) speckled brown
- ⅛ oz (4 g) blue

Height: 2 in (5 cm)

See also

Pastes, icings, glues, pages 28–33 > Modeling techniques, pages 42–47 > Designing your figures, pages 48–51

2 For the neck, shape a white pinch of paste into a flat disk, approximately ½ in (1.2 cm) in diameter. Attach to the front of the duck using edible glue and dry spaghetti. Allow the strand to stand out of the neck ready to support the head.

3 Make the head from the green paste. Shape into a dome. Form a slight neck, allowing most of the paste to remain as a ball shape. Use the flower veining tool to accentuate the neck by creasing slightly. Flatten the eye area slightly. Attach to the body using dry spaghetti and a dab of edible glue. Add two tiny black paste eyes.

1 For the body, shape 2 oz (56 g) brown paste into an egg shape, the curved end being the front of the duck. Taper the pointed end and square off slightly. Make the base of the duck broader than the top.

4 For the beak, roll the orange paste into a cone shape, soften the top, and, using the small palette knife, mark the mouth. Use the flower veining tool to mark the nostrils on the beak. Attach to the head using dry spaghetti and edible glue.

5 The feathers are made the same way, but in varying sizes and colors. Roll a teardrop with the appropriate paste, flatten, and, using the flower veining tool, draw it down the paste to texture it. Attach the paste to the duck using dots of royal icing. This will allow the feathers to stick to the body, but not so that they look flat.

6 Start by applying the lowest black feathers, working up through the layers: white next, then another black feather. From this point, move forward and attach the cream side feathers, bringing them forward so that most of the side of the duck is feathered. Above this cream feather is the white-blue-white block of feathers. Now, attach the peach tail feather at the back of the duck. Next, attach the large brown side feathers, and finally the speckled brown back feather.

39 ostrich

Long, thin legs support a large, heavy body—this is quite difficult to pull off with paste, so this ostrich chick is sitting down.

Materials

- Modeling paste
- Gum paste
- Corn starch
- Dry spaghetti
- Edible glue
- Shortening
- 3-in (7.5-cm) length of 22 ga. pink wire

Tools

- Workboard
- Rolling pin
- Flower veining tool
- Clay gun with multi-hole disk
- X-acto knife
- Tennis ball

Colors Used

- 2½ oz (70 g) gray modeling paste
- 2 oz (56 g) white gum paste
- 1¼ oz (35 g) white
- 1 oz (28 g) yellow
- ● Pinch black

Height: 3 in (8 cm)

See also
Pastes, icings, glues, pages 28–33 > Modeling techniques, pages 42–47 > Designing your figures, pages 48–51

6 Attach two tiny eyes made from pinches of black paste.

5 The head and neck are made as one piece, using 1 oz (28 g) white modeling paste. Shape the wire into the finished shape. Roll the paste into a sausage, leaving one end more bulbous. Thread the paste down the wire, leaving some wire bare. Insert into the body of the ostrich, using edible glue to secure in place. Push the neck section up against the body, again using edible glue. Allow the head to sit at the top of the wire, bent over slightly. Support in place until dry.

4 Make two identical wings from ½ oz (14 g) gray modeling paste. Shape into two teardrops, flatten, and, using the flower veining tool, indent down one side of the shape. Attach in place using edible glue.

3 Make the tufts of feather by placing a pinch of white paste, mixed with shortening, into the clay gun and extruding the paste through the multihole disk. Attach in place using edible glue.

7 Shape the beak from the remaining yellow paste. Shape a triangle, but bevel the base to fit the shape of the face. Attach in place with edible glue.

8 Add hair to the head following the instructions in Step 3, using the rest of the white modeling paste.

9 Make the egg shell from the white gum paste. Roll it out thinly, cut out a large circle, and use the X-acto knife to create a jagged edge. Wrap the paste around a ball (a tennis ball is ideal, but remember to sterilize with boiling water and leave to dry for 24 hours, and to dust with corn starch). Let the paste dry on the ball for 24 hours.

1 Shape 2 oz (56 g) gray modeling paste into an egg shape for the body. Narrow the end. Use the flower veining tool to create tail feathers.

2 Make the legs and feet from the yellow paste, reserving just a pinch for the beak. Shape two elongated teardrops and push dry spaghetti into the narrow end, in preparation for the feet. Shape the feet into two broad teardrops, flatten the shape, and, using the flower veining tool, indent the broad end to create "toes." Attach the feet to the legs and the legs to the body, using edible glue to secure in place.

40 parrot

This is an amazingly striking bird, suitable for beginners as well as advanced fondant modelers.

Materials

- Modeling paste
- Corn starch
- Dry spaghetti
- Edible glue
- Royal icing

Tools

- Workboard
- Rolling pin
- Iris petal cutter
- Oval cutter
- Small palette knife
- Paper towel

Colors Used

- ● 5 oz (140 g) red
- ● 2½ oz (70 g) gold
- ● 1 oz (28 g) blue
- ○ ¼ oz (7 g) white
- ● Pinch black

Height: 3½ in (9 cm)

See also
Pastes, icings, glues, pages 28–33 > Modeling techniques, pages 42–47 > Props, pages 248–253

4 Shape the head from 2 oz (56 g) red paste. Roll into a cylinder, softening one end for the back of the head. Bend slightly and attach to the body using edible glue. If the head is overbalanced and topples over, set the head further back.

5 Roll out ¼ oz (7 g) white paste. Use the oval cutter to cut two white oval sections for the face. Attach with edible glue. Add eyes by rolling two black balls from the black paste.

6 Shape the beak from 1 oz (28 g) gold paste. Shape into a cone and, using the small palette knife, firmly indent the mouth. Attach to the head using edible glue and dry spaghetti. Support the beak in place until dry using paper towel.

3 Attach the wings in the same way as in Step 2. Start with the lowest feather sitting at the extreme of length you want to create. Attach with royal icing.

2 Roll out 1 oz (28 g) each of the red, gold and blue paste, fairly thinly. Use the iris petal cutter to cut out several feathers for the tail and wings. Start by placing the first feather at the extreme length for the tail. This will be the furthest point. Attach to the elongated body using a dot of royal icing. Continue adding feathers with royal icing, building up the tail until you are happy with the effect.

1 For the body, shape 2 oz (56 g) red paste into a rough horseshoe with a fat middle and thinner end sections. Insert dry spaghetti through the neck section ready for the head. Graduate the depth of the tail section and elongate.

7 Add a gold chest to the parrot using the remaining gold paste. Roll into a ball, flatten, and roll again slightly with the rolling pin. Attach in place using edible glue.

41 peacock

Sparkly petal dust highlights the fabulous coloring of this beautiful bird.

Materials

- Modeling paste
- Corn starch
- Edible glue
- Sparkly petal dust

Tools

- Workboard
- Rolling pin
- Paper towel
- Pizza cutter
- Flower veining tool
- Petal cutter
- Dusting brush

Colors Used

- 4 oz (112 g) blue
- 1 oz (28 g) green
- ¼ oz (7 g) yellow
- Pinch white
- Pinch black
- Pinch orange

Height: 2¾ in (7 cm)

See also
Pastes, icings, glues, pages 28–33 > Color mixing, pages 38–39 > Modeling techniques, pages 42–47

2 Take a pinch of white paste and shape into two eyes. Attach to either side of the head. Add two black pupils. Roll two tiny blue sausage shapes for each eye, to act as eyelids, and attach around the eyeball on each side, securing in place with edible glue.

3 Make the peacock comb from balls of paste: large yellow balls, medium green balls, and small blue balls. Balance the balls on top of each other using edible glue to secure in place. Hold for a few seconds until secure.

1 Make the body and beginnings of the tail using 3 oz (84 g) blue paste. Roll into a long teardrop, lengthen for the neck, and flatten the broader end, smoothing it into a long tail. Bend up the neck and curve over the very top for the head. Support in this position until dry using paper towel.

4 Add a tiny beak made from a pinch of orange paste. Roll into a cone and attach to the head using edible glue.

5 For the wings, roll ½ oz (14 g) blue paste into two balls, lengthen into a rough teardrop shape, and flatten with the rolling pin. Reshape with the pizza cutter if required and then score the wings using the pointed end of the flower veining tool to represent the feathers. Attach around each side of the body with edible glue.

7 Finish the peacock by painting the blue parts of the tail feathers and the wings with a sparkly petal dust.

6 Roll out the green paste thinly and use the petal cutter to cut the feathers for the tail. Decorate each one with a yellow disk and a smaller blue disk half over the yellow one. Attach to the tail feathers using edible glue. Attach the tail feathers to the peacock using edible glue, making the tail as long and full as you wish.

42 penguin

The contrasting black, white and yellow of this charming Emperor Penguin are very striking.

Materials

- Modeling paste
- Corn starch
- Edible glue
- Dry spaghetti
- Sunflower petal dust

Tools

- Workboard
- Rolling pin
- Paper towel
- X-acto knife
- Pizza wheel
- Dusting brush

Colors Used

- 1⅛ oz (32 g) white
- ¾ oz (21 g) black
- Pinch gold

Height: 3¾ in (9.5 cm)

See also

Pastes, icings, glues, pages 28–33 > Color mixing, pages 38–39 > Modeling techniques, pages 42–47

6 Roll some of the gold paste into two elliptical shapes, flatten and attach to the beak.

5 Shape the head and nose into a teardrop from ⅛ oz (4 g) of black paste. Attach the head to the body using edible glue and dry spaghetti.

4 Roll out ⅛ oz (4 g) black paste and flatten with the rolling pin. Use the pizza wheel to cut out an oval shape, then use the X-acto knife to cut a triangle out of one end. Trim the two points to neaten. Wrap around the back of the body, allowing the tail section to overlap the tail of the body. Use edible glue to attach in place.

3 Roll out ⅛ oz (4 g) black paste into a long, thin sausage, then flatten and roll. Cut two elliptical shapes for the wings from the black paste, and cut one pointed end off. Attach to each side of the penguin.

2 Shape the body from 1 oz (28 g) white paste. Roll into a cylinder and flatten one end to make a tail. Stand the cylinder on the flattened end. Tuck the feet under the end and secure with edible glue. Support using paper towels until dry.

7 Make the hair from pinches of gold, white and black paste. Roll the paste in the palm of one hand, shaping into small sausages that taper at both ends. Bend in half, then secure in place on the head with edible glue.

8 Add the eyes to the penguin using two pinches of black paste. Secure in place with edible glue.

9 Finish by adding two oval disks made using the rest of the white paste to the neck area of the penguin. Attach with edible glue, then dust them with the sunflower petal dust and dusting brush. Dust down the side of the chest area, too.

1 Make the feet from ⅛ oz (4 g) black paste. Roll into two cylinders, flatten, and, using the X-acto knife, cut two triangles out of the flattened end to create three webbed toes.

43 toucan

The large beak of this exotic bird will need supporting until dry.

Materials

- Modeling paste
- Corn starch
- Edible glue
- Dry spaghetti
- Dowelling rods (optional)
- Green florist's tape (optional)

Tools

- Workboard
- Rolling pin
- Flower veining tool

Colors Used

- ● 2¾ oz (77 g) black
- ● 1½ oz (42 g) orange
- ○ ¾ oz (21 g) white
- ● ½ oz (14 g) yellow
- ● ¼ oz (7 g) brown

Height: 3½ in (9 cm)

See also
Pastes, icings, glues, pages 28–33 > Modeling techniques, pages 42–47 > Designing your figures, pages 48–51

3 Roll out the white paste and cut a rough oval shape. Attach the bottom of the shape to the front of the bird, wrapping it around to the head section to allow the toucan to be looking backward.

4 Shape the orange paste into a cone and flatten a little, marking the upper and lower beak with the end of the flower veining tool. Attach to the face using dry spaghetti and edible glue. Support until set.

2 Shape the wings from ½ oz (14 g) black paste. Make two teardrops and texture with the flower veining tool, drawing lines up from the edge. Attach to the body with edible glue.

1 Shape 2 oz (56 g) black paste into an egg. Narrow the neck section slightly, flatten the base, and stretch out a little from the base to create a tail. Use the flower veining tool to texture the tail. Indent the end to create a scallop shape.

6 For the feet, shape the brown paste into two teardrops, flatten, and indent using the flower veining tool. Attach to the base of the body. The bird can sit on a twig if desired. Use doweling rods wrapped in green florist's tape.

5 Shape the yellow paste into two flat disks for the eyes. Attach to the face, then add a dot of black paste for the pupil. Secure as before.

44 british robin

This cheery chap would brighten up any cake.

Materials
- Modeling paste
- Corn starch
- Edible glue

Tools
- Workboard
- Rolling pin
- Bone tool
- Flower veining tool
- X-acto knife

Colors Used
- 1¾ oz (49 g) white
- ¼ oz (7 g) red
- ¼ oz (7 g) brown
- Pinch black

Height: 3 in (8 cm)

See also
Pastes, icings, glues, pages 28–33 > Modeling techniques, pages 42–47 > Designing your figures, pages 48–51

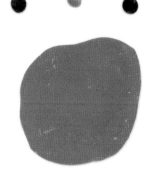

3 Indent the head with the bone tool. Insert two eyes made from two rolled balls of black paste. Attach with edible glue.

2 Shape the red breast by flattening the red paste and softening the edges on the workboard. Attach to the body using edible glue.

4 Using a pinch of brown paste, shape a beak. Mark down each side using the flower veining tool and attach with edible glue.

1 Shape the body into a softened cone using the white paste.

5 Make the back and tail feathers from the rest of the brown paste. Shape into a long teardrop, flatten using the rolling pin, and texture with the flower veining tool. Use the X-acto knife to trim a few triangles of paste from the bottom of the teardrop, to represent the tail feathers. Attach to the body and head using edible glue.

45 rubber duck

A cute rubber duck, perfect for a beginner modeler. Here, we used marzipan, but you can make this model from any number of pastes.

Materials

- Modeling paste
- Marzipan
- Corn starch
- Edible glue
- Dry spaghetti
- Edible white paint

Tools

- Workboard
- Rolling pin
- Flower veining tool
- Paint brush

Colors Used

- 3½ oz (98 g) yellow marzipan
- ½ oz (14 g) orange marzipan
- ¼ oz (7 g) white
- Pinch black

Length: 5 in (13 cm)

See also
Pastes, icings, glues, pages 28–33 > Modeling techniques, pages 42–47 > Designing your figures, pages 48–51

4 Shape the head from 1 oz (28 g) yellow marzipan. Roll into a ball and attach using edible glue and dry spaghetti.

5 Shape the beak from the orange marzipan. Shape into an oval, flatten one end, and curve the broad end. Use the flower veining tool to texture and to mark the nostrils. Attach the flat end to the face using edible glue.

6 Add two eyes. Start with two white balls flattened onto the face, then add two black balls on top. Secure with edible glue.

3 For the wings, roll ½ oz (14 g) yellow marzipan into two teardrop shapes, flatten, and indent the long side with the flower veining tool to create the edge feathers. Attach to the sides with edible glue.

7 Paint a white dot on each pupil using the edible white paint.

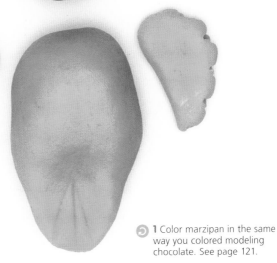

2 Shape 2 oz (56 g) yellow marzipan into a teardrop. Flatten the pointed end and texture the tail with the flower veining tool. Lift the tail so it is at a perky angle.

1 Color marzipan in the same way you colored modeling chocolate. See page 121.

46 swan

Two elegant swans to grace any sophisticated cake.

Materials

- Modeling paste
- Corn starch
- Edible glue
- Black, red and blue edible paints
- Silver petal dust

Tools

- Workboard
- Rolling pin
- Flower veining tool
- Paper towel
- Pizza cutter
- Paint brush
- Dusting brush

Colors Used

● 3 oz (84 g) white

Length: 2¾ in (7 cm)

See also
Pastes, icings, glues, pages 28–33 > Color mixing, pages 38–39 > Modeling techniques, pages 42–47

2 Shape the remaining white paste into two wings. Roll out into an oval, shaping slightly to a point at one end, and using the pizza cutter to trim. Score the wings using the flower veining tool. Attach the wings to the sides of the body with edible glue, supporting with rolls of paper towel until they are able to hold their own shape.

3 Paint the face on the swan using the edible paint.

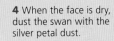

4 When the face is dry, dust the swan with the silver petal dust.

1 Shape the neck, head and body from one piece of white paste. Use 2½ oz (70 g). Shape into a long teardrop, elongating the neck and narrowing the head. Broaden the tail end, pinching the very end where the tail feathers are. Use the flower veining tool to score the tail feathers. Bend the neck up into the classic swan shape and support in place using paper towel until dry. Pinch the beak to sharpen slightly.

47 puffin

The distinctive beak of this popular bird make it instantly recognizable.

Materials

- Modeling paste
- Corn starch
- Dry spaghetti
- Edible glue
- Shortening

Tools

- Workboard
- Rolling pin
- Pizza cutter
- X-acto knife
- Ball tool
- Flower veining tool
- Clay gun

Colors Used

- 3½ oz (98 g) black
- 2¾ oz (77 g) white
- 1 oz (28 g) red
- Pinch yellow

Height: 3¾ in (9.5 cm)

See also
Pastes, icings, glues, pages 28–33 > Modeling techniques, pages 42–47 > Designing your figures, pages 48–51

4 Roll out ½ oz (14 g) white paste. Cut out a large oval using the pizza cutter and trim to give a sharp point at one end. Cut off the other end to give a flat end. Indent the eye socket using the ball tool and draw a line using the pointed end of the flower veining tool, from the eye socket to the point of the white face section. Attach to the head using edible glue with the flat end nearest to where the beak will be.

5 Shape 1 oz (28 g) of red paste into a sharp triangular shape to make the beak. Curve the broad base and indent so it fits neatly up against the face and flush up with the white face section. Attach with edible glue.

3 Make the head from 1 oz (28 g) black paste. Roll into an egg shape. Attach to the body using dry spaghetti and edible glue. Leave to dry.

6 Add two black triangles made from pinches of black paste. Allow to dry. Add shortening to ¼ oz (7 g) white paste and put it into a clay gun. Extrude a string of white paste and attach this around the black section of the beak and around the white facial section, cutting and fitting using the X-acto knife. Attach with edible glue. Add a dot of yellow paste to either side of the beak.

2 Roll out 2 oz (56 g) black paste for the black section of the back and tail feathers and shape into a teardrop. Trim using the pizza cutter. Cut the tail feather section using the X-acto knife. Place over the white body, allowing it to drape over the shape. Smooth with your hands, securing in place with edible glue.

1 Shape the body from 2 oz (56 g) white paste. Shape into a teardrop, but flatten the narrow end, leaving the neck end broad. Insert dry spaghetti ready to support the head.

7 Finish by making two wings from ½ oz (14 g) black paste. Roll into two oval shapes, flatten, and score down the oval with the flower veining tool. Secure against either side of the body with edible glue.

48 woodpecker

Make the tip of the beak nice and sharp for this woodpecker to be able to peck away.

Materials

- Modeling paste
- Corn starch
- Edible glue
- Dry spaghetti
- Mid-green petal dust

Tools

- Workboard
- Rolling pin
- Flower veining tool
- Pizza cutter
- X-acto knife
- Dusting brush

Colors Used

- 6 oz (168 g) pale green
- ½ oz (14 g) red
- ¼ oz (7 g) black
- Pinch white

Length: 4½ in (11 cm)

See also
Pastes, icings, glues, pages 28–33 > Color mixing, pages 38–39 > Modeling techniques, pages 42–47

5 Roll out ¼ oz (7 g) black paste and, using the flower veining tool, cut a strip approximately ¼ in (6 mm) wide. Attach this across the front of the face, just before the start of the beak, securing it with edible glue.

6 Add eyes to the black band. Make two white eyeballs from two pinches of white paste, then add two tiny black balls using edible glue to secure in place.

7 Finish the head by rolling out the red paste and cutting a long oval shape. Attach this from the front of the face to the back of the neck, with edible glue to secure.

4 Roll out ½ oz (14 g) green paste and, with the pizza cutter, cut an oval disk and attach onto the back of the head. Score with the flower veining tool to represent feathers.

8 Make two feet from ½ oz (14 g) green paste. Roll into a sausage, flatten, and, using the X-acto knife, cut three toes, trimming to make the foot section quite narrow. Tuck under the body and secure with edible glue.

3 For the head and beak, shape 1 oz (28 g) green paste into an elongated teardrop and attach to the body using edible glue and dry spaghetti. Support in place until dry.

2 For the tail feathers, roll out 1 oz (28 g) green paste and cut a rectangular shape. Using the X-acto knife, trim one end to a point and indent for the tail feathers. Attach to the back, positioned so that the head will cover it. Attach with edible glue.

9 For the wings, shape 1 oz (28 g) green paste into a teardrop and flatten. Texture with the flower veining tool. Attach to the body using edible glue.

10 Dust the bird with a mid-green petal dust.

1 For the body, shape 2 oz (56 g) green paste into a curved sausage. Flatten one end and score with the pointed end of the flower veining tool. Bend up the other end of the body. Support until dry.

49 bush baby

The large round eyes of this bush baby make him extra sweet.

Materials

- Modeling paste
- Corn starch
- Edible glue
- Dry spaghetti
- Black petal dust
- Pink petal dust

Tools

- Workboard
- Rolling pin
- Flower veining tool
- X-acto knife
- Decorating tip No. 1
- Dusting brush

Colors Used

- 4½ oz (126 g) gray
- ½ oz (14 g) gold
- Pinch black
- Pinch pink

Height: 3½ in (9 cm)

See also
Pastes, icings, glues, pages 28–33 > Color mixing, pages 38–39 > Modeling techniques, pages 42–47

4 For the head, mold 1 oz (28 g) gray paste into a fat teardrop, drawing the narrow end forward for the muzzle. Indent the eye sockets with the broad end of the flower veining tool. Mark a mouth using the end of the decorating tip. Add a tiny pink nose and secure with edible glue. Secure the head to the body using dry spaghetti and edible glue. Dust the eye sockets well with black petal dust.

5 Roll two eyes from the gold paste, flatten, and secure in place with edible glue. Add two black pupils and secure in the same way.

6 Shape the ears from ½ oz (14 g) gray paste. Roll into two balls, flatten, and thin along the outside edge until you have ears that are large and thin with a thick center. Attach to the head using edible glue. Dust the outside of the ears with black petal dust, and the inside with pink petal dust.

1 Shape the body from 1½ oz (42 g) gray paste. Mold into an egg shape, the pointed end being the head end. Score the body with the flower veining tool to represent fur.

3 Roll ½ oz (14 g) gray paste into two teardrops for the front legs, flattening the narrow end and marking the fingers as before. Score the fatter end roughly for fur, then attach to the body using edible glue.

2 For the back legs, roll 1 oz (28 g) gray paste into elongated teardrops. Flatten the narrow end and mark the fingers of the bush baby using the X-acto knife. Bend the legs back to form the knee, then bend forward again to form the recognizable shape of the back legs. Attach to the body using edible glue. Score the paste using the flower veining tool.

camel

This beautiful beast would make a fine feature on a desert-themed cake.

Materials

- Modeling paste
- Corn starch
- Edible glue
- Dry spaghetti
- Light brown petal dust

Tools

- Workboard
- Rolling pin
- Ball tool
- Small palette knife
- Flower veining tool
- Paper towel
- Dusting brush

Colors Used

6¼ oz (175 g) cream
● Pinch black

Height: 5 in (12 cm)

See also
Pastes, icings, glues, pages 28–33 > Color mixing, pages 38–39 > Modeling techniques, pages 42–47

2 For the head and neck, roll 2 oz (56 g) cream paste into a sausage, making one end slightly narrower; this will be the head end. Bend at the top of the neck and shape the face, indenting the eye socket with the end of the ball tool and the mouth with the small palette knife. Add a nose from a pinch of cream paste, shaped into a triangle and indented with the end of the flower veining tool. Bend a small amount of paste at the bottom of the neck. Tuck this part under the body and secure using edible glue. Support the head with paper towel until dry.

3 Roll two pinches of cream paste into teardrops for the ears and indent the center with the flower veining tool. Attach to the head with edible glue.

4 Roll pinches of cream paste in the palm of your hand into mini banana shapes for the eyelids. Attach to the face with edible glue. Insert pinches of black paste into the sockets, securing with edible glue.

1 For the body, shape 2 oz (56 g) cream paste into a cone, sharpen the lower edge, and soften the top of the cone.

5 Make four legs from 1 oz (28 g) cream paste. Roll out thinly and insert dry spaghetti through the center of each leg. Roll to make a little thinner, allowing the spaghetti to extend beyond the leg at both ends. Allow to dry.

8 Dust the camel with a light brown petal dust to add depth.

6 For the feet, roll four balls from 1 oz (28 g) cream paste and indent the front of each with the flower veining tool. Push the legs onto the feet, using edible glue to secure. Leave to dry. Attach under the body, positioning them so that the camel body and head are balanced.

7 Roll a pinch of cream paste into a sausage for the tail.

lion

Not so much King of the Jungle, this lion's too sweet for that.

Materials

- Modeling paste
- Corn starch
- Edible glue
- Dry spaghetti

Tools

- Workboard
- Rolling pin
- Flower veining tool
- Small palette knife
- Ball tool

Colors Used

- 3 oz (84 g) gold
- 1¼ oz (35 g) gold/brown
- Pinch black

Length: 3½ in (9 cm)

See also
Pastes, icings, glues, pages 28–33 **>** Modeling techniques, pages 42–47 **>** Designing your figures, pages 48–51

4 Make the head from ½ oz (14 g) gold paste, shape into a teardrop, flatten the point for the top of the head, and narrow the middle section of the shape. Mark the eyes on the narrow section using the flower veining tool and mark the muzzle on the broad section using the small palette knife. Attach to the mane using the prepared dry spaghetti and edible glue.

5 For the eyes, roll a pinch of black paste into two tiny balls and attach to the head using edible glue. Shape the nose from a pinch of gold/brown paste. Shape into a pyramid and attach to the muzzle using edible glue. Mark the mouth with the small palette knife, indent the ends with the small end of the ball tool, and prick the muzzle with end of the flower veining tool.

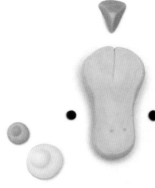

3 The mane is made from 1 oz (28 g) gold/brown paste. Pinch off a small amount for the ears and nose. Roll the rest into a ball and flatten. Score several times from the center out using the pointed end of the flower veining tool. Attach to the body using edible glue. Push dry spaghetti through the mane and into the body, leaving a little protruding for the head.

6 Make the ears from two pinches of gold paste. Roll into balls and indent the center using the ball tool. Attach the ears to the head. Line the ears with two tiny pinches of gold/brown paste.

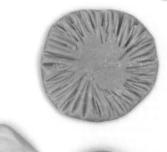

2 Shape the body from 1 oz (28 g) gold paste. Roll into an oval and attach to the legs using dry spaghetti and edible glue.

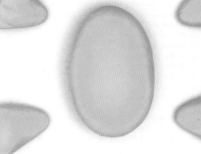

1 Make the legs and feet first by rolling 1 oz (28 g) gold modelling paste into four balls. Shape the balls into cones. Mark the paws using the pointed end of the flower veining tool. Attach the legs together with edible glue and leave to dry.

7 Shape the tail from ⅛ oz (4 g) gold paste. Roll into a sausage that is thinner at one end than the other, and attach the broad end to the body using edible glue.

giraffe

Make your giraffe's neck as long as you like.

Materials

- Modeling paste
- Corn starch
- Dry spaghetti
- Edible glue
- Shortening

Tools

- Workboard
- Rolling pin
- Flower veining tool
- Decorating tip No. 1
- Ball tool
- Clay gun

Colors Used

- 6½ oz (182 g) cream
- 2 oz (56 g) brown (more if desired)
- Pinch black

Height: 6 in (15 cm)

See also

Pastes, icings, glues, pages 28–33 > Modeling techniques, pages 42–47 > Designing a cake, pages 52–53

4 For the head, roll 1 oz (28 g) cream paste into a teardrop, but flatten the narrow end for the top of the head. Indent the nose using the pointed end of the flower veining tool. Mark the mouth with the end of the decorating tip and the small end of the ball tool. Attach two tiny balls of the black paste for the eyes using edible glue.

3 For the neck, roll 1 oz (28 g) cream paste into a sausage. Push dry spaghetti down the neck so they protrude from both ends, one end longer than the other. Attach to the body by the longer end, using edible glue to assist. Support until dry.

2 For the body, roll 2 oz (56 g) cream paste into a slightly flattened, oval shape and allow to dry a little. Attach to the legs using a little edible glue and the dry spaghetti.

1 For the legs, roll 2 oz (56 g) cream paste into a long sausage shape. Cut into four equal length legs, approximately 2 in (5 cm) long. Push dry spaghetti through each one so it protrudes at both ends. Make four hooves from 1 oz (28 g) brown paste. Roll the paste into a ball, flatten slightly, and indent with the flower veining tool. Attach to the legs by applying edible glue and pushing onto the leg. Stick the legs together and leave to dry.

5 For the ears, roll two pinches of cream paste into a teardrop, flatten, and draw the flower veining tool across to indent. Attach to the head using edible glue.

6 For the ossicones, roll two tiny pinches of cream paste into sausages. Trim the ends to flatten, then attach to the head using edible glue. Make two tiny balls using the brown paste, flatten, and attach to the top of the ossicones using edible glue.

7 Make the brown spots from different-sized balls of brown paste and flatten to give different-sized spots. Attach using edible glue.

8 Add shortening to ½ oz (14 g) brown paste and extrude through the clay gun to create strands of paste. Cut to size and attach to the giraffe using edible glue.

53 gorilla

For instructions on how to make the banana, see page 249.

Materials

- Modeling paste
- Corn starch
- Dry spaghetti
- Edible glue

Tools

- Workboard
- Rolling pin
- Flower veining tool
- Paper towel
- Small palette knife
- Ball tool
- X-acto knife

Colors Used

- 4½ oz (126 g) brown
- 2¾ oz (77 g) cream
- Pinch white
- Pinch black

Height: 5 in (12 cm)

See also
Pastes, icings, glues, pages 28–33 > Modeling techniques, pages 42–47 > Props, pages 248–253

6 For the muzzle, roll ½ oz (14 g) cream paste into a ball, flatten one side, and attach the flat side to the head with edible glue. Mark the mouth with the small palette knife. Deepen the mouth and indent the nostrils with the flower veining tool. Shape the eyebrow section by adding a pinch of cream paste rolled into a flattened oval. Attach to the head above the muzzle. Use the smaller end of the ball tool to indent the eye sockets and accentuate the eyebrows.

5 Make the head from 1 oz (28 g) brown paste. Roll into a cone shape, flatten the top, and attach to the body with edible glue and dry spaghetti.

4 For the arms, shape 1 oz (28 g) brown paste into two sausages, slightly thinner than the legs. Attach to the body using edible glue, bending at the elbows and resting them on the legs.

3 For the legs, shape 1 oz (28 g) brown paste into two fat sausage shapes, bend at the knee, and flatten a little at one end to tuck under the body. Secure in place using edible glue. Support the knees with rolled-up paper towel to hold the shape until set.

2 For the chest, shape 1 oz (28 g) cream paste into a heart, softening the edges. Attach to the body using edible glue. Mark the nipples using the pointed end of the flower veining tool.

7 For the ears, roll two pinches of cream paste into two balls, flatten the center with the small end of the ball tool, and attach to the head using edible glue. Add two eyeballs using a pinch of white paste attached with edible glue, and two pupils with a pinch of black paste.

8 Make two hands and two feet from 1 oz (28 g) cream paste, ¼ oz (7 g) for each one. Roll into a teardrop, flatten, and, using the X-acto knife, cut four slits to create five digits. Use the flower veining tool and your fingers to soften and shape. Cut a flat end for the wrist and attach to the arms and legs using edible glue.

1 Shape the body from 1½ oz (42 g) brown paste. Make the paste into a cone and soften the edges. Insert dry spaghetti into the neck.

hippo

This cute little hippo is begging to be put on top of your cake.

Materials

- Modeling paste
- Corn starch
- Edible glue
- Dry spaghetti
- Light silver luster dust

Tools

- Workboard
- Rolling pin
- Scallop tool
- Flower veining tool
- Bone tool
- X-acto knife
- Dusting brush
- Paper towel

Colors Used

- 3 oz (84 g) pink
- Pinch white
- Pinch black
- Pinch cream

Length: 2¼ in (5.5 cm)

See also
Pastes, icings, glues, pages 28–33 > Modeling techniques, pages 42–47 > Designing your figures, pages 48–51

4 Shape the head from 1 oz (28 g) pink paste. Shape into an egg shape and flatten the narrow end to form the top of the head. Mark the mouth and the nostrils, and divide the muzzle using the pointed end of the flower veining tool. Again with the pointed end of this tool, indent the muzzle several times. Attach the head to the body using edible glue and dry spaghetti. Attach two tiny balls of pink paste for the nostrils.

3 Make the front legs in the same way, using ⅛ oz (4 g) of pink paste for each leg, but make them thinner and shorter. Attach to the body using edible glue and create creases using the flower veining tool.

5 Shape two teeth from two pinches of white paste. Shape into a square and attach to the face with edible glue.

6 Form the eyes out of two tiny pinches of white paste, rolled into a ball and flattened. Attach with edible glue. Overlay with two tiny pinches of black paste for the pupils.

7 Roll two pinches of pink paste into balls, flatten with the bone tool to indent, and attach to the head with edible glue.

8 Make the bow from two pinches of cream paste. Roll each into a teardrop. Cut off the pointed end using the X-acto knife, then use the flower veining tool to indent the sides. Attach to the head, flat ends together. Then, roll a further pinch of cream paste into a ball, flatten slightly and attach over the join with edible glue.

2 Shape each back leg from ¼ oz (7 g) of pink paste. Roll into a cylinder, then squash one end slightly to make it a little fatter. Mark the nails with the scallop texture tool, then attach to the body using edible glue. Use the flower veining tool to add creases at the join with the body.

9 With the remaining pink paste, roll into a long cone for the tail. Attach to the body with the point upward, using edible glue.

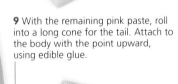

1 Shape the body from 1 oz (28 g) pink paste. Make an egg shape, with the fatter end slightly flattened. Place the shape onto the workboard, flattened end down, so it sits up at an angle.

10 Dust the hippo with light silver luster dust. Use the brush to dust the hippo by putting a little dust onto the paper towel, loading your brush from there, then tapping off the excess before dusting your animal.

55 kangaroo and joey

Try the kangaroo first, then add baby roo; he's made of similarly shaped pieces but is smaller.

Materials

- Modeling paste
- Corn starch
- Edible glue
- Dry spaghetti

Tools

- Workboard
- Rolling pin
- Flower veining tool

Colors Used

- 4½ oz (126 g) chestnut
- Pinch black

Height: 4 in (10 cm)

See also
Pastes, icings, glues, pages 28–33 > Modeling techniques, pages 42–47 > Props, pages 248–253

2 For the head, shape ½ oz (14 g) chestnut paste into a teardrop, flatten the narrow end, and pinch in the central part to create the nose. Mark the eye sockets, nose and mouth using the flower veining tool. Attach to the body using edible glue and dry spaghetti pushed through the neck section of the body.

3 Shape the eyes and nose from small pinches of black paste. Roll two tiny balls for the eyes. Shape the nose from a slightly larger pinch of paste. Attach with edible glue.

4 For the ears, roll ⅛ oz (4 g) chestnut paste into two teardrops, flatten, and soften the central section of the ear using the flat end of the flower veining tool. Cut off the point and attach the ears to the head using edible glue, holding in place for a few minutes until they stay.

5 For the arms roll ⅛ oz (4 g) chestnut paste into two small sausages, approximately 1 in (2.5 cm) long. Indent the end of the arms using the pointed end of the flower veining tool to represent fingers. Attach to the body using edible glue.

1 For the body, roll 2 oz (56 g) chestnut paste into an elongated oval. Extend one end for the tail, leaving the central section broader. Lengthen the opposite end for the body and neck, then bend gently into the desired shape. Stand the shape up and support until dry.

7 Create the joey by making the same shapes as the kangaroo for the body, head, ears and arms. Use a pinch of chestnut paste for each one. Eyes and nose are also made the same way but with smaller quantities of black paste. Attach the body to the front of the kangaroo with edible glue. For the pouch, roll out ⅛ oz (4 g) chestnut paste and cut an oval shape, then cut off one end. Attach to the body using edible glue, covering three-quarters of the joey's body. Attach the head parts together as before.

6 Finish the kangaroo by making the back legs using 1 oz (28 g) chestnut paste. Shape into two teardrops; flatten the point on the teardrop, but extend the length to give the leg shape. Flatten the shape slightly and bend the broader section over. Attach to the body using edible glue and mold to the shape of the kangaroo.

56 koala

Don't you just want to give this koala a hug?

Materials

- Modeling paste
- Corn starch
- Edible glue
- Dry spaghetti
- Black petal dust

Tools

- Workboard
- Rolling pin
- Flower veining tool
- Dusting brush

Colors Used

○ 1½ oz (42 g) gray
● Pinch black

Height: 2¼ in (6 cm)

See also

Pastes, icings, glues, pages 28–33 > Color mixing, pages 38–39 > Modeling techniques, pages 42–47

5 Make the eyes from two tiny pinches of black paste rolled into balls. Attach with edible glue. Use a larger pinch for the nose. Roll into an oval and attach to the head using edible glue.

6 Make the ears from two pinches of gray paste. Roll into a ball and flatten. Use the flattened end of the flower veining tool to thin the center of the ball. Cut a little off one side to give a flat end, and attach this end to the head of the koala, one on either side of the head.

4 The head is shaped from ½ oz (14 g) gray paste. Roll into a ball and flatten one side slightly to give a flatter area for the back of the head. Mark the eyes using the end of the flower veining tool. Attach the head to the body using edible glue and dry spaghetti.

7 Finish the koala by making tufts of fur to add to the ears. Roll tiny balls of gray paste into thin sausage shapes, fold in half, and attach to the head in front of the ears using edible glue.

3 Shape the upper limbs in exactly the same way with the same volume of paste.

2 The back legs are made from ⅛ oz (4 g) gray paste. Shape two back legs by rolling two small, oval-shaped sausages. Use the pointed end of the flower veining tool to indent one end of each for digits. Attach to the base of the body using edible glue. Position the legs so they face in the same direction, as if the koala were holding onto a tree.

8 Dust the koala with black petal dust to accentuate the back of the bear, the arms, and the tips of the hair.

1 Shape the body from ½ oz (14 g) gray paste. Roll into a ball, flatten the base slightly, and flatten the tummy section a little.

elephant

Here is a sweet little female elephant. You could turn it into a male by making a pale blue bow and wrapping it around the neck.

Materials

- Modeling paste
- Corn starch
- Edible glue
- Dry spaghetti

Tools

- Workboard
- Rolling pin
- Scallop tool
- Small palette knife
- Bone tool
- Round cutter
- Pizza cutter
- Paper towel
- Flower veining tool

Colors Used

- 4¾ oz (133 g) gray
- ¼ oz (14 g) pink
- Pinch white
- Pinch black

Height: 3½ in (9 cm)

See also
Pastes, icings, glues, pages 28–33 > Modeling techniques, pages 42–47 > Designing your figures, pages 48–51

5 Add ears to the head using ½ oz (14 g) gray paste. Roll out into a rough round shape and, using the round cutter, cut a round out. Using the cutter again, cut two elliptical shapes. Attach the ears to the head using edible glue.

6 For the bow, roll out the pink paste into a long sausage. Flatten and neaten using the pizza cutter to leave a ribbon of paste. Cut in half and fold the two strips over to make loops. Use a roll of paper towel to support the loops if necessary. Attach to the head using edible glue. With the remnants of the pink paste, make the knot for the bow. Attach as before. Indent the bow using the flower veining tool to represent folds.

4 Add eyes to the head. First attach two balls of white paste to the head using edible glue, then add two tiny black pupils with edible glue.

3 The head and trunk are made from 1 oz (28 g) gray paste. Roll into a teardrop but elongate the thinner end. Shape the end of the trunk and the mouth using the small palette knife. Indent the eye sockets using the small end of the bone tool. Attach to the body using edible glue and dry spaghetti.

7 Finish the model by adding a tail. Roll ¼ oz (7 g) of gray paste into a long thin sausage. Indent one end for the tassel. Attach to the body using edible glue.

2 Shape the body from 2 oz (56 g) gray paste. Roll into a ball and attach to the legs using edible glue and dry spaghetti.

1 Make the feet and legs from 1 oz (28 g) gray paste. Roll into a cylinder and cut into four equal parts. Indent the toes using the scallop tool. Allow to dry.

58 meerkat

These meerkats are standing up on their back legs, taking in their fondant-covered surroundings.

Materials

- Modeling paste
- Corn starch
- Edible glue
- Dry spaghetti
- Chestnut brown petal dust

Tools

- Workboard
- Rolling pin
- Flower veining tool
- Ball tool
- Small palette knife
- Dusting brush

Colors Used

3¾ oz (106 g) light brown

⅛ oz (4 g) white

● Pinch black

Height: 5 in (13 cm)

See also
Pastes, icings, glues, pages 28–33 > Modeling techniques, pages 42–47 > Props, pages 248–253

4 Make two eyes from two pinches of black paste and attach to the head with edible glue.

3 Shape ½ oz (14 g) light brown paste into a teardrop with a pointed top for the head. Indent the eye sockets with the ball tool and attach the head to the body using edible glue and dry spaghetti. Mark the mouth with the side of the small palette knife.

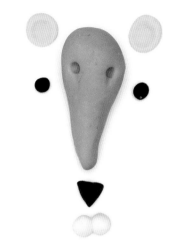

5 Make the ears from two pinches of light-brown paste. Shape into balls, flatten the center with the smaller end of the ball tool, and attach to the head with edible glue.

2 Shape the legs from ½ oz (14 g) light brown paste. Roll out four thin sausage shapes; two for the arms and two for the legs. Attach the arms to the top of the cone, curving them around the body and down to create the typical meerkat pose. Mark the paws with the end of the flower veining tool. Attach the lower legs under the body shape with edible glue. Mark the paws as before, but make them more pronounced.

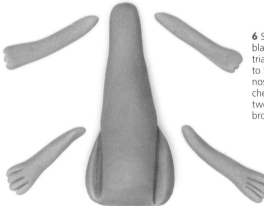

6 Shape a pinch of black paste into a triangle and attach to the end of the nose. Attach two cheeks made from two balls of light brown paste.

1 For the body, roll 2 oz (56 g) light brown paste into a tall cone. Mark the back legs using the flower veining tool. Roll out ⅛ oz (4 g) white paste into an elongated oval. Cut one end off and attach to the front of the body using edible glue.

7 Finish by dusting the meerkat with chestnut brown petal dust, paying close attention to the eyes and ears.

59 orangutan

The hands and feet of this orangutan make him extra expressive.

Materials

- Modeling paste
- Corn starch
- Dry spaghetti
- Edible glue
- Shortening

Tools

- Workboard
- Rolling pin
- Flower veining tool
- X-acto knife
- Ball tool
- Small palette knife
- Clay gun

Colors Used

- 5 oz (140 g) terracotta
- 1½ oz (42 g) brown
- ½ oz (14 g) light terracotta
- Pinch black

Height: 5 in (12 cm)

See also
Pastes, icings, glues, pages 28–33 > Modeling techniques, pages 42–47 > Designing your figures, pages 48–51

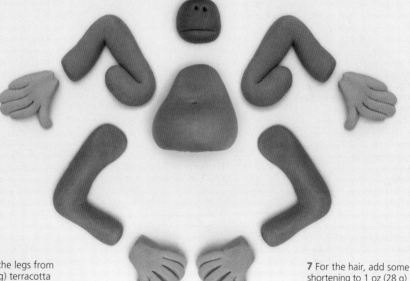

4 For each hand, roll ¼ oz (7 g) light terracotta paste into a teardrop, flatten, and, using the X-acto knife, cut four slits to create five digits. Use the flower veining tool and your fingers to soften and shape. Cut a flat end for the wrist and attach to the arms and legs using edible glue.

3 For the arms, roll 1 oz (28 g) terracotta paste into two long sausages. Curl over ¼ in (6 mm) at one end for the shoulders, bend in the center for the elbows, and use the flower veining tool to add creases. Attach to the body allowing the curled over part to jut up, giving the orangutan its distinctive posture.

5 For the head, roll 1 oz (28 g) brown paste into a ball. Use the small end of the ball tool to indent the eye sockets. Use the flower veining tool to accentuate the eyebrows. Attach to the body with edible glue and dry spaghetti. Make sure it sits quite low down so that the shoulders look hunched.

6 For the muzzle, shape ½ oz (14 g) brown paste into a ball, flatten, and mark the nostrils with the end of the flower veining tool. Mark the mouth with the small palette knife. Attach to the front of the head with edible glue. Add two tiny black balls for eyes.

2 Shape the legs from 1 oz (28 g) terracotta paste. Make an elongated teardrop, cut off the point, flatten the broader end slightly, and tuck under the body of the orangutan. Bend the legs. Use the flower veining tool to make creases at the knees.

1 For the body, shape 2 oz (56 g) terracotta paste into a cone. Use the flat end of the flower veining tool to flatten the chest and accentuate the tummy. Indent the tummy button. Push dry spaghetti through the neck to support the head.

7 For the hair, add some shortening to 1 oz (28 g) terracotta paste and extrude through the clay gun to create multiple strands. Attach to the head using edible glue.

panda

Everyone loves a panda, and this cartoon-style interpretation is very cute.

Materials

- Modeling paste
- Corn starch
- Edible glue
- Dry spaghetti

Tools

- Workboard
- Rolling pin
- Flower veining tool
- X-acto knife
- Decorating tip No. 1
- Small palette knife
- Bone tool

Colors Used

- 4¼ oz (119 g) white
- 2¾ oz (77 g) black

Height: 3½ in (9 cm)

See also
Modeling techniques, pages 42–47 > Designing your figures, pages 48–51 > Props, pages 248–253

6 Make the eyes by rolling out a small amount of black paste. Use the end of the decorating tip to cut out the patches. Make two white eyeballs out of small balls of white paste and attach over the top of the black patches using edible glue. Add two tiny pupils using black paste and secure as before.

5 Make the head from ½ oz (14 g) white paste. Roll into a ball and attach to the body using dry spaghetti.

7 Shape the muzzle from ¼ oz (7 g) white paste. Shape into a ball and attach to the front of the face using edible glue. Mark the mouth with the end of the decorating tip. Add a black nose with a ball of black paste, shaped into a rough triangle, and attach with edible glue.

4 For the arms, roll ½ oz (14 g) black paste into two sausage shapes, flatten slightly at one end for the hand, thinning the opposite end to wrap around the back of the panda. Mark the paws using the pointed end of the flower veining tool. Attach using edible glue.

3 Roll ¼ oz (7 g) black paste into a circular shape. Trim if necessary using the X-acto knife. Attach this black patch to the top of the body, overlapping front and back to give a black top to the body. Use edible glue to attach.

2 For the back legs, shape 1½ oz (42 g) black paste into two cylinders, curve each one round slightly and tuck under the body. Secure with edible glue.

1 For the body, mold 3¼ oz (91 g) white paste into a ball, then press gently to flatten the base. Use the flower veining tool to indent the tummy a little.

8 Use ¼ oz (7 g) black paste to make two ears. Shape into a ball, cut in half with the small palette knife, flatten the half balls a little, and use the bone tool to indent the inside of the ears. Attach with edible glue.

zebra

A cute addition to a jungle-themed cake.

Materials

- Modeling paste
- Corn starch
- Dry spaghetti
- Edible glue
- Shortening

Tools

- Workboard
- Rolling pin
- Decorating tip No. 1
- Flower veining tool
- Clay gun
- Pizza cutter

Colors Used

- 3 oz (84 g) white
- 2¼ oz (63 g) black

Height: 4½ in (11 cm)

See also
Modeling techniques, pages 42–47 > Designing your figures, pages 48–51 > Props, pages 248–253

4 For the head, shape ½ oz (14 g) white paste into a rough teardrop with a flattened top. Use the big end of the decorating tip to mark the mouth at the broad end. Mark two eye sockets using the end of the flower veining tool. Make nostrils by rolling two tiny balls of white paste, attach to the muzzle using edible glue, and indent using the end of the flower veining tool. Attach the head to the body using the dry spaghetti and edible glue.

5 Make two tiny eyes with black paste, securing to the face with edible glue.

6 Shape the ears from two tiny pinches of white paste rolled into a teardrop. Flatten the center with the flat end of the flower veining tool and attach to the head with edible glue.

7 Take ½ oz (14 g) black paste, add some shortening, and knead well. Put into the clay gun and extrude through the multihole disk to create the mane. Attach to the head using edible glue.

3 For the body, roll 1½ oz (42 g) white paste into a ball and push onto the dry spaghetti of the legs. (You might want to dab edible glue onto each leg first.) Push dry spaghetti through the front of the body, ready for the head.

2 Roll 1 oz (28 g) black paste into four equal balls for the hooves. Attach one to the bottom of each leg, securing with edible glue. Shape the front two black balls into hoofs. Leave to dry.

8 Roll ⅛ oz (4 g) white paste into a long, thin sausage for the tail. Attach to the body using edible glue. Add a tiny dot of black paste for the end of the tail.

1 For the legs, roll ¾ oz (21 g) white paste into a long cylinder of approximately 4 in (10 cm) in length and cut into four equal pieces. Push dry spaghetti through each one so that it protrudes from both ends. Attach all four legs together using edible glue.

9 Use the remaining black paste to create stripes. Roll it thinly, then cut stripes using the pizza cutter. Attach to the zebra with edible glue.

62 tiger

Make some of the props on pages 248–253 to place this tiger in his natural habitat.

Materials

- Modeling paste
- Corn starch
- Edible glue
- Dry spaghetti

Tools

- Workboard
- Rolling pin
- Flower veining tool
- Ball tool
- Small palette knife

Colors Used

- 5½ oz (154 g) orange
- ¾ oz (21 g) white
- ½ oz (14 g) black
- ¼ oz (7 g) pink

Length: 3½ in (9 cm)

See also
Pastes, icings, glues, pages 28–33 > Modeling techniques, pages 42–47 > Designing your figures, pages 48–51

3 For the ears, take a pinch of orange paste, roll it into a ball, and flatten. Cut in half and indent each semicircle using the end of the ball tool. Attach to the head using edible glue.

2 For the head, shape 1 oz (28 g) orange paste into a triangle and flatten the two side points for the fur at the side of the face. Use the flower veining tool to texture. Indent the eyes using the end of the flower veining tool. Attach to the body using edible glue and dry spaghetti. Add two tiny eyes made from black paste.

1 For the body, shape 2 oz (56 g) orange paste into an egg and flatten the pointed end.

8 Add a tail using the remaining orange paste rolled into a long sausage. Attach with edible glue and add stripes as before.

4 For the muzzle, roll ½ oz (14 g) white paste into two balls and attach together. Attach to the face and prick with the end of the flower veining tool. Add a mouth made with a tiny pinch of white paste, shaped like a banana. Add a nose made with the pink paste, shaped into a pyramid and indented with the flower veining tool. Attach all with edible glue.

5 For the front legs, shape 1 oz (28 g) orange paste into two teardrops. Tuck the narrow end under the head, securing with edible glue, then texture the paws with the end of the flower veining tool.

6 For back paws, shape 1 oz (28 g) orange paste into a teardrop, flatten, and indent part way along to shape the narrow end into a foot. Attach to the side of the body with edible glue, pressing firmly. Indent the paws with the flower veining tool.

7 Make the stripes for the tiger by rolling pinches of black paste in the palm of your hand. Flatten and attach to the tiger with edible glue. Do the same for the white stripes on the face and the black stripes on the head.

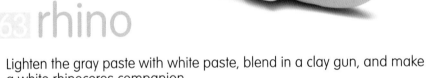

63 rhino

Lighten the gray paste with white paste, blend in a clay gun, and make a white rhinoceros companion.

Materials

- Modeling paste
- Corn starch
- Dry spaghetti
- Edible glue
- Light pink petal dust

Tools

- Workboard
- Rolling pin
- Flower veining tool
- Ball tool
- Dusting brush

Colors Used

- 7¼ oz (203 g) gray
- Pinch black

Height: 4 in (10 cm)

See also
Pastes, icings, glues, pages 28–33 > Color mixing, pages 38–39 > Modeling techniques, pages 42–47

4 Shape the two horns from ½ oz (14 g) gray paste. Roll one tiny, cone-shaped horn and use the remaining paste for the larger horn. Attach to the head using edible glue, using the flower veining tool to score and create creases at the base.

5 Shape the ears from two pinches of gray paste. Roll a teardrop and flatten the center. Cut off a little paste from the broad end to leave a flat end to attach to the head.

6 Make the neck creases from 1 oz (28 g) gray paste. Shape into a tapered sausage, flatten, and score with the flower veining tool. Attach to the back of the head and top of the body using edible glue. Allow the ends to drape round and under the chin. Texture further.

3 For the head, shape 1½ oz (42 g) gray paste into a rough rectangle. Use the small end of the ball tool to indent the nostrils. Pull the tool up slightly to create bulges of paste above the nostril. Indent sockets for the eyes. Make two tiny balls from the black paste and secure in the eye sockets using edible glue. Attach the head to the body using the dry spaghetti. Allow the mouth of the rhino to rest on the workboard.

2 For the body, shape 2 oz (56 g) gray paste into an egg and attach to the feet using edible glue. Insert dry spaghetti for the head. Attach tiny slivers of gray paste to the top of each leg with edible glue and use the flower veining tool to score.

1 For the feet, roll 2 oz (56 g) dark gray paste into a long sausage and cut into four pieces. Flatten and squash slightly to crease. Mark the toes using the flower veining tool. Insert dry spaghetti through each to support the body.

7 Finish the rhino with a pinch of gray paste rolled into a thin sausage for the tail. Attach with edible glue.

8 Dust the rhino with a little light pink petal dust.

polar bear

A polar bear in a hat and scarf? It must be cold!

Materials

- Modeling paste
- Corn starch
- Dry spaghetti
- Edible glue

Tools

- Workboard
- Rolling pin
- Ball tool
- Paper towel
- Pizza cutter
- Bone tool
- Flower veining tool

Colors Used

- 3¾ oz (105 g) white
- ½ oz (14 g) pale blue
- Pinch black

Height: 4 in (10 cm)

See also
Pastes, icings, glues, pages 28–33 > Modeling techniques, pages 42–47 > Designing your figures, pages 48–51

5 Shape the ears from two ⅛ oz (4 g) balls of white paste. Indent the center using the small end of the bone tool. Attach to the head using edible glue.

4 For the scarf, roll ¼ oz (7 g) pale blue paste into a long sausage, flatten with the rolling pin, and texture by rolling over the paste with a piece of textured paper towel. Use the pizza cutter to trim to a length of approximately 2 in (5 cm) by ¼ in (6 mm). Wrap around the neck and secure with edible glue. Make two pompoms by rolling two pinches of white paste, indent with the bone tool, and attach to the ends of the scarf with edible glue.

3 The head is shaped from ½ oz (14 g) white paste. Form a teardrop shape. Flatten the point to create a nose. Attach the head to the body using edible glue and dry spaghetti. Indent the eye sockets with the small end of the ball tool.

2 Make the body from 1½ oz (42 g) white paste. Shape into an oval and attach to the legs using edible glue and the dry spaghetti in the legs. Push dry spaghetti through one end of the body ready for the head.

6 Shape the woolly hat from the remaining pale blue paste. Make a cone and indent one side to create a crease using the flower veining tool. Attach to the head using edible glue. Add a pompom, made as before. Make a band of white paste the same way as the scarf. Attach with edible glue.

7 Add the eyes and nose to the head. Use two tiny pinches of black paste for the eyes and a triangle of the remaining black paste for the nose, and attach using edible glue.

1 For the legs and feet, roll 1 oz (28 g) white paste into four equal balls, then shape into a cylinder, broaden, and fatten the base for the foot. Push dry spaghetti into each foot, with a small amount protruding. Leave to dry.

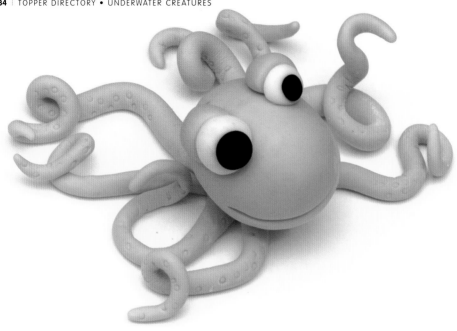

65 octopus

Have fun arranging this octopus's legs into all sorts of unusual positions.

Materials
- Modeling paste
- Corn starch
- Edible glue
- Dry spaghetti
- Green petal dust

Tools
- Workboard
- Rolling pin
- Paper towel
- Flower veining tool
- Bone tool
- Dusting brush

Colors Used
- 5¼ oz (147 g) green
- Pinch white
- Pinch black

Height 2¾ in (7 cm)

See also
Pastes, icings, glues, pages 28–33 > Color mixing, pages 38–39 > Modeling techniques, pages 42–47

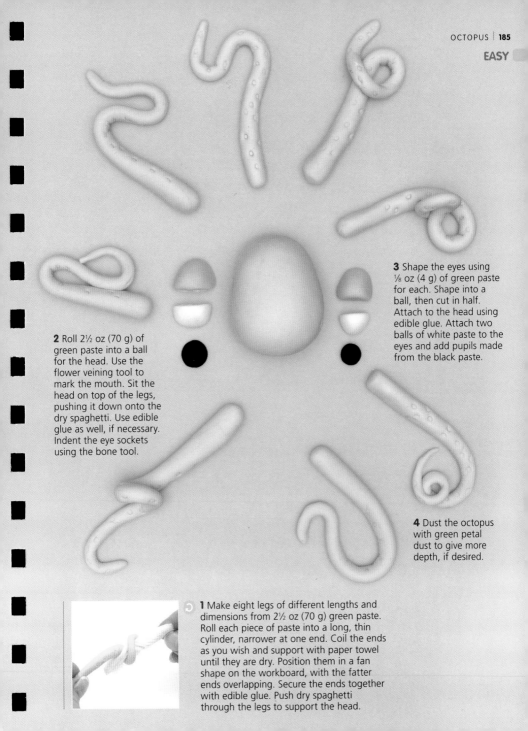

3 Shape the eyes using ⅛ oz (4 g) of green paste for each. Shape into a ball, then cut in half. Attach to the head using edible glue. Attach two balls of white paste to the eyes and add pupils made from the black paste.

2 Roll 2½ oz (70 g) of green paste into a ball for the head. Use the flower veining tool to mark the mouth. Sit the head on top of the legs, pushing it down onto the dry spaghetti. Use edible glue as well, if necessary. Indent the eye sockets using the bone tool.

4 Dust the octopus with green petal dust to give more depth, if desired.

1 Make eight legs of different lengths and dimensions from 2½ oz (70 g) green paste. Roll each piece of paste into a long, thin cylinder, narrower at one end. Coil the ends as you wish and support with paper towel until they are dry. Position them in a fan shape on the workboard, with the fatter ends overlapping. Secure the ends together with edible glue. Push dry spaghetti through the legs to support the head.

66 crab

This friendly fellow would go well on a birthday cake for someone born under the zodiac sign of Cancer.

Materials

- Modeling paste
- Corn starch
- Edible glue
- Seven 4½-in (11-cm) pieces of 24 ga. wire
- Dry spaghetti

Tools

- Workboard
- Rolling pin
- Flower veining tool
- Bone tool
- X-acto knife

Colors Used

- 5 oz (140 g) orange
- Pinch white
- Pinch black

Length: 3 in (8 cm)

See also
Pastes, icings, glues, pages 28–33 > Modeling techniques, pages 42–47 > Designing your figures, pages 48–51

2 Cut one of the pieces of wire in half and dust with orange petal dust. Attach two tiny balls of orange paste to one end and attach them to the body. Make two larger balls of orange paste and attach to the other end. Add a white eyeball and a black pupil to each eye, securing everything in place with edible glue.

3 For each leg, bend a piece of wire equally twice to give three sections. Roll a pinch of orange paste into a teardrop, then insert the end of the wire into the pointed end, pushing the paste up to the first bend. Roll another pinch of paste into a teardrop and insert this down the wire, threading from the fatter end this time. Push down the wire to meet the paste already in position. Do the same with a final pinch of paste. Push each leg into the indentations down the side of the body and secure in place with edible glue.

4 Make the claws from ⅜ oz (11 g) of orange paste. Shape into a ball, then an oval, and flatten. Thin and narrow one end of the oval to make a "wrist" for the claw. Use the X-acto knife to cut out a "V" shape to sharpen the end of the claw. Insert dry spaghetti into the claws, cover the spaghetti with orange paste, and insert the strands into the front of the body. Allow them to rest on the workboard until dry.

1 Shape the body from 3½ oz (98 g) of orange paste. Shape into a ball, then flatten to create a squashed oval. Mark the mouth using the flower veining tool. Open the mouth slightly. Mark the nostrils. Using the bone tool, make three indentations down each side of the body in preparation for the legs.

67 goldfish

Fancy this swimming around your goldfish bowl?

Materials

- Modeling paste
- Corn starch
- Edible glue

Tools

- Workboard
- Rolling pin
- Flower veining tool
- Ball tool
- Pizza cutter

Colors Used

- 4 oz (112 g) pale orange
- 1 oz (28 g) dark orange
- 2 pinches white
- Pinch black

Length: 3 in (8 cm)

See also
Pastes, icings, glues, pages 28–33 > Modeling techniques, pages 42–47 > Designing your figures, pages 48–51

4 Roll two tiny pinches of pale orange paste for the lips. Roll into a sausage, pointing each end. Wrap around the mouth using edible glue to attach.

5 Take the white paste, roll into two balls, and attach to the face for two eyeballs. Add two tiny black balls for pupils.

3 Make the long hair from ½ oz (14 g) dark orange paste in the same way as the stripes, but pinch in the middle, then attach to the head using edible glue. To make the short spikey hair, roll small cones in the palm of your hand, then attach on top of the longer hair, using edible glue and allowing it to stand up.

6 Using 1¼ oz (35 g) of the pale orange paste, shape into two small fins and one large fin. Roll into a teardrop and, using the pointed end of the flower veining tool, score the paste toward the point. Attach the two small fins either side of the body, and the large one on top using edible glue.

2 Take ½ oz (14 g) dark orange paste, roll thinly, and, using the pizza cutter, cut strips that are broad in the center. Attach to the body using edible glue.

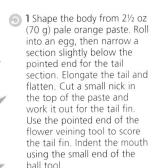

1 Shape the body from 2½ oz (70 g) pale orange paste. Roll into an egg, then narrow a section slightly below the pointed end for the tail section. Elongate the tail and flatten. Cut a small nick in the top of the paste and work it out for the tail fin. Use the pointed end of the flower veining tool to score the tail fin. Indent the mouth using the small end of the ball tool.

68 clown fish

This cheerful clown fish would brighten any child's birthday cake.

Materials

- Modeling paste
- Corn starch
- Edible glue

Tools

- Workboard
- Rolling pin
- Scallop tool
- Bone tool
- Flower veining tool

Colors Used

- 2¾ oz (77 g) orange
- 1 oz (28·g) white
- Pinch black

Length: 4¾ in (12 cm)

See also
Pastes, icings, glues, pages 28–33 > Modeling techniques, pages 42–47 > Props, pages 248–253

3 Make three small fins out of the orange paste, about ⅛ oz (4 g) each. Then make one medium ¼ oz (7 g) fin and one ⅜ oz (11 g) tail. To do this, roll the orange paste balls into a cone and then flatten. Texture with the flower veining tool by drawing it along the paste. Pinch one end to make a fan shape. Cut off the point.

4 Roll a pinch of black paste in the palm to taper. Attach one of these to the ends of each fin with edible glue. Secure the flat ends of the fins to the body.

5 Roll out 1 oz (28 g) white paste thinly. Cut into strips of varying widths and attach to the body using edible glue.

1 Using 1½ oz (42 g) orange paste, shape the body into an elongated comma. Use the scallop tool to mark the scales on the body of the fish. Indent the eyes with the bone tool and mark the mouth.

2 Make the eyes from small pinches of white paste. Roll into balls and attach with edible glue. Add pupils with a pinch of black paste and fix in place with edible glue.

seal

A delightful, cute creature.

Materials
- Modeling paste
- Corn starch
- Edible glue
- Flower stamens
- Edible black paint

Tools
- Workboard
- Rolling pin
- X-acto knife
- Ball tool
- Flower veining tool
- Paint brush

Colors Used
- 3 oz (84 g) white
- Pinch black

Height: 3½ in (9 cm)

See also
Pastes, icings, glues, pages 28–33 > Modeling techniques, pages 42–47 > Designing your figures, pages 48–51

4 Push two tiny black paste balls into the eye sockets. Secure with edible glue.

3 For the head, roll 1 oz (28 g) white paste into an egg shape. Attach to the head using edible glue. Indent the face with the narrow end of the ball tool to create eye sockets.

2 Make the front paws by rolling ¼ oz (7 g) into two teardrop shapes. Indent the broad end to create paws. Attach the narrow end to the shoulder of the body. Curl the paws in front of the body.

1 For the body, shape 1 oz (28 g) white paste into a teardrop. Flatten the narrow end, and cut up the center using an X-acto knife. Flatten each fin and curl backward slightly. Bend the tail fin upward and support in place until set.

5 Attach a tiny pinch of white paste for the mouth. Roll into a cigar shape and attach to the bottom of the cheeks with edible glue.

6 For the cheeks, roll ¼ oz (7 g) white paste into two tiny balls. Flatten one side and attach to the nose section. Prick with the pointed end of the flower veining tool. Insert flower stamens into the cheeks for the whiskers.

7 For the nose, shape a pinch of black paste into a pyramid and attach to the top of the cheeks with edible glue.

8 Paint around the nose using a dry brush and edible black paint to give a slightly gray color. Paint the center of the mouth also.

70 shark

This caricature-style shark wears lipstick and blush, but you can make your own shark as scary or as tame as you like.

Materials

- Modeling paste
- Corn starch
- Edible glue
- Edible white paint
- Pink petal dust

Tools

- Workboard
- Rolling pin
- X-acto knife
- Flower veining tool
- Ball tool
- Paint brush
- Dusting brush

Colors Used

- 2¾ oz (77 g) light blue
- 1 oz (28 g) pink
- ½ oz (14 g) white
- Pinch black

Length: 6 in (15 cm)

See also
Pastes, icings, glues, pages 28–33 > Color mixing, pages 38–39 > Modeling techniques, pages 42–47

4 Shape the pink paste into two sausages, tapered at each end, approximately 2½ in (6 cm) long. Indent the middle of the upper lip using the flower veining tool. Attach to the front of the shark with edible glue.

3 Roll two balls from ½ oz (14 g) white paste and insert into the eye sockets, securing in place with edible glue. Add two pinches of black paste for pupils and attach as before. Roll two eyebrows from two pinches of black paste and attach over the eyes with edible glue. Paint a dot in each black pupil with edible white paint.

5 Shape two flippers from ½ oz (14 g) blue paste. Shape into teardrops, curling over the top slightly. Attach to the sides of the shark with edible glue.

6 Dust the cheeks with pink petal dust until you are happy with the depth of color.

2 Shape the dorsal fin from ¼ oz (7 g) blue paste and attach to the top of the shark with edible glue.

1 Shape 2 oz (56 g) blue paste into a teardrop. Cut the narrow end using the X-acto knife and separate the two parts. Flatten and texture with the flower veining tool. Bend the tail section up and support in place until dry. Indent the eye area with your fingers to create a shelf of paste. Indent with the fat end of the ball tool to create two sockets. Indent two nostrils using the pointed end of the flower veining tool.

siamese fighting fish

A very flamboyant fish with an amazing, flowing tail.

Materials

- Modeling paste
- Corn starch
- Edible glue

Tools

- Workboard
- Rolling pin
- Scallop tool
- Pizza cutter
- Flower veining tool
- Paper towel

Colors Used

- 4 oz (112 g) pale lilac
- ¾ oz (21 g) dark lilac
- ⅛ oz (4 g) white
- Pinch black

Length: 4¾ in (12 cm)

See also
Pastes, icings, glues, pages 28–33 > Modeling techniques, pages 42–47 > Designing your figures, pages 48–51

1 Make the body of the fish from 2 oz (56 g) pale lilac paste. Shape into an egg shape, then arch the backbone area by flattening and softening either side. Use the scallop tool to create the scales and indent the mouth and gills.

6 Make the dorsal fin from ½ oz (14 g) pale lilac. Shape into a long sausage and flatten, leaving one long side slightly fatter than the other. Score with the flower veining tool from the fatter side to the thinner side. Attach to the backbone using edible glue and use a paper towel to support until dry.

2 Shape the pale lilac part of the tail fin first. Roll out 1 oz (28 g) of paste thinly at one end, leaving the other end a little thicker. Score with the pizza cutter and flower veining tool. Use the pizza cutter to trim to an even shape. Ripple the paste slightly and allow to dry. Attach the narrower, fatter end to the body using edible glue and support in place with paper towel until dry. Do the same using all of the dark lilac paste, attaching one or two pieces.

5 Make the front fins from ½ oz (14 g) pale lilac paste. Roll into two teardrops. Flatten and splay out the bulbous end, leaving the pointed end a little thicker. Use the flower veining tool to score. Attach to either side with edible glue.

4 Roll two pinches of pale lilac paste so that they are thin at each end but fatter in the middle. Attach to the mouth using edible glue.

3 Shape the eyes from the white paste. Roll into two teardrops and attach to the head using edible glue. Add two black pupils and attach them in the same way.

EASY

sea life

An anemone and three different types of shell make up an enchanting sea-themed cake.

SEA ANEMONE

1 Shape 1 oz (28 g) paste into a cylinder, sharpening the edges.

2 Roll out ½ oz (14 g) paste thinly and cut a strip using the pizza cutter that is as broad as the cylinder. Wrap this around the cylinder, cutting off the excess with the X-acto knife and securing in place using edible glue.

3 Use the remaining paste to make the tentacles by rolling pinches of paste in the palm of your hand, leaving one end fatter and the other really thin.

SHELLS

1 All the shells are made the same way, just with varying amounts of paste. Shape the paste into an elongated cone, very thin at one end and slowly getting broader.

2 Starting with the narrow end, begin rolling the paste up. Secure in place as you work along the shape using edible glue. Allow the coil to protrude as you work along the shape, giving you the shell shape.

3 Scoring the elongated cone using the flower veining tool will give you the pattern shown on the cream shell.

Materials/Tools	Colors Used
• Modeling paste • Corn starch • Workboard • Rolling pin • Pizza cutter • X-acto knife • Edible glue	● 2 oz (56 g) pale blue **Height: 1¼ in (3 cm)**

Materials/Tools	Colors Used
• Modeling paste • Corn starch • Workboard • Rolling pin • Edible glue • Flower veining tool	1 oz (28 g) cream ● ½ oz (14 g) pale brown ¼ oz (7 g) white **Length: 1 in (2.5 cm)**

74 starfish

This is a very simple, but attractive, addition to a cake.

1 Separate the paste into five equal parts and shape each part into a sausage that is slightly thinner at one end than the other.

2 Using the X-acto knife, trim the fatter end to a point, so that each of the five legs of the starfish will slot together, securing each one with edible glue.

3 Texture each leg with the end of the decorating tip.

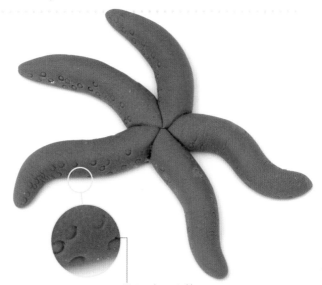

Texture is created by pressing the end of the decorating tip into the paste.

Materials

- Modeling paste
- Corn starch
- Edible glue

Tools

- Workboard
- Rolling pin
- X-acto knife
- Decorating tip No. 4

Colors Used

● 1 oz (28 g) jade green

Width: 4 in (10 cm)

See also
Pastes, icings, glues, pages 28–33 **>** Modeling techniques, pages 42–47 **>** Props, pages 248–253

INTERMEDIATE

seahorse

The head, body and tail of this fish are made from just one piece of paste.

Attach the fins to the body with edible glue.

1 Shape 1¾ oz (49 g) gold paste into a long sausage. Graduate the thickness of the paste. The middle should be the thickest; the top end should be thinner, but not as thin as the tail end.

2 Roll the tail section first, coiling it neatly forward.

3 Allow the fattest part to be the chest area. Bend the paste at 90 degrees to the body to create the head. Narrow the head to a point around the nose, then flare it slightly to create the mouth.

4 Make indentations down the back of the seahorse with the flower veining tool. Texture the body and head using the end of the decorating tip.

5 Make the fins from about ¼ oz (7 g) of gold paste. Roll into a ball, flatten into a fan shape and, using the flower veining tool, texture the fins. Attach to the back of the sea horse with edible glue.

6 Use two pinches of the remaining gold paste to form the eyes. Attach to the top of the head followed by a flattened disk of white paste for each eye and two pupils made from black paste.

Materials

- Modeling paste
- Corn starch
- Edible glue

Tools

- Workboard
- Rolling pin
- Flower veining tool
- Decorating tip No. 4

Colors Used

- 2 oz (56 g) gold
- Pinch white
- Pinch black

Height: 4½ in (11 cm)

See also
Pastes, icings, glues, pages 28–33 > Modeling techniques, pages 42–47 > Props, pages 248–253

dolphin

These intelligent, friendly and playful animals are very popular.

Use the flower veining tool to give the tail fin texture.

1 Roll 2 oz (56 g) of blue paste into a sausage shape. Lengthen and thin the nose end and taper the opposite end, flattening it out for the tail fin. Mark the eye positions and the mouth using the flower veining tool. Shape the tail fin using the X-acto knife and mark it with the flower veining tool.

2 Make three fins from the remaining ½ oz (14 g) blue paste. For each one, shape the paste into a ball, then into a triangular shape with softened edges. Attach to the top and to either side of the body.

3 Make the eyes from a pinch of black paste.

Secure in place using edible glue.

4 Paint the lower section of the head and mouth with edible white paint.

Materials

- Modeling paste
- Corn starch
- Edible glue
- Edible white paint

Tools

- Workboard
- Rolling pin
- Flower veining tool
- X-acto knife
- Paint brush

Colors Used

2½ oz (70 g) blue
● Pinch black

Length: 6 in (15 cm)

See also
Pastes, icings, glues, pages 28–33 > Color mixing, pages 38–39 > Modeling techniques, pages 42–47

77 turtle

The petal-dusted cheeks of this turtle give him extra character and charm.

Materials

- Modeling paste
- Corn starch
- Edible glue
- Green petal dust
- Pink petal dust

Tools

- Workboard
- Rolling pin
- Bone tool
- Flower veining tool
- Dusting brush

Colors Used

- 2¼ oz (63 g) brown
- 2 oz (56 g) white
- 1⅛ oz (32 g) pale green
- 1 oz (28 g) pale yellow
- Pinch black

Length: 6 in (15 cm)

See also
Color mixing, pages 38–39 > Modeling techniques, pages 42–47 > Designing your figures, pages 48–51

3 Use ½ oz (14 g) pale green paste for the head. Shape into a teardrop, but flatten the point and thicken it into a neck shape. Bend the head to one side and indent the eye sockets with the bone tool. Place to one side.

4 Add two tiny eyes to the head using two tiny dots of black paste. Attach in place using edible glue.

2 Shape the body from 2 oz (56 g) white paste. Shape into a ball, then flatten. It should be slightly wider and slightly shorter than the lower shell. Place on top of the lower shell, but don't secure in place yet.

5 Make the legs from ½ oz (14 g) pale green paste. Roll into four balls, shape into cones, lengthen the legs slightly, and place on top of the lower shell at the four corners along with the head. Secure in place using edible glue. Secure the body on top.

1 For the lower shell, roll 1 oz (28 g) pale yellow paste into a ball and knead to soften. Roll into a sausage and flatten using the rolling pin. Shape so that one end is pointed and the other more rounded.

8 Finish by dusting with green and pink petal dust to add depth and character to the turtle.

6 Use the brown paste to make the upper shell. Pinch off a ball of paste, shape into a rough square, and attach to the body using edible glue. Repeat, outlining the outside of the shell before working in and pushing each square together neatly. Use the flower veining tool to adjust, if necessary. As you work up the shell, you may need to cut triangles, but shape in the same way as before.

7 Make the tail from the remnants of pale green paste and attach to the back of the lower shell using edible glue.

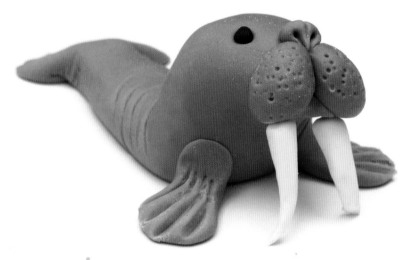

walrus

This walrus might be a somber fellow, but he's full of character.

Materials

- Modeling paste
- Corn starch
- Edible glue
- Dry spaghetti

Tools

- Workboard
- Rolling pin
- X-acto knife
- Flower veining tool
- Bone tool
- Paper towel

Colors Used

- 4 oz (112 g) brown
- ⅛ oz (4 g) white
- Pinch black

Length: 2¾ in (7 cm)

See also
Pastes, icings, glues, pages 28–33 > Modeling techniques, pages 42–47 > Designing your figures, pages 48–51

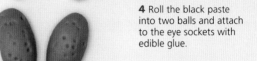

3 Shape the nose and muzzle using ½ oz (14 g) brown paste. Pinch a little off this for the nose. Roll into a ball, flatten the base, then score up the center with the flower veining tool. Indent the nostrils with this tool also. Place to one side. Shape the remaining paste into two ovals, flatten slightly, and attach to the face using edible glue. Prick the muzzle with the pointed end of the flower veining tool. Attach the nose in the same way.

4 Roll the black paste into two balls and attach to the eye sockets with edible glue.

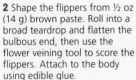

2 Shape the flippers from ½ oz (14 g) brown paste. Roll into a broad teardrop and flatten the bulbous end, then use the flower veining tool to score the flippers. Attach to the body using edible glue.

1 Shape the body, head and tail from 3 oz (84 g) brown paste. Roll into a tapered sausage, the head end being fatter than the tail end. Slice approximately 1 in (2.5 cm) through the tail using the X-acto knife. Shape the tail with your fingers and then use the flower veining tool to score the tail. Indent the eyes with the end of the bone tool, then bend the head up and use the paper towel to support until dry.

5 To make the tusks, roll the white paste into two elongated teardrops. Push dry spaghetti into the fatter end of the teardrop, add a dab of edible glue onto this end, and insert the spaghetti into the head under the muzzle. Push the tusks up and attach to the head.

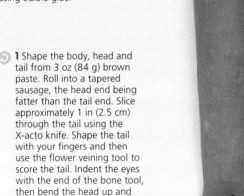

whale

A simple shape for a beginner to make. The more experienced might want to add texture to the fins and add petal dust to create depth and interest.

Materials

- Modeling paste
- Corn starch
- Edible glue
- Dry spaghetti

Tools

- Workboard
- Rolling pin
- X-acto knife
- Paper towel
- Flower veining tool

Colors Used

- 4 oz (112 g) gray
- ⅛ oz (4 g) white
- Pinch black

Length: 5½ in (14 cm)

See also
Pastes, icings, glues, pages 28–33 > Modeling techniques, pages 42–47 > Designing your figures, pages 48–51

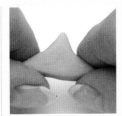

3 Shape the two side fins from ½ oz (14 g) gray paste. Roll into two triangles, soften the corners, and stretch the point slightly backward to give the distinctive fin shape.

2 Shape the pale underbelly of the whale using the white paste. Shape into a teardrop, flattening and reshaping it. Attach to the underside of the whale using edible glue. Score the white sides of the whale using the flower veining tool.

4 Make two balls from the black paste for the eyes. Secure in place on the head using edible glue.

5 Finish with the dorsal fin using ½ oz (14 g) gray paste. Shape as before for the fins and attach to the top of the whale using edible glue.

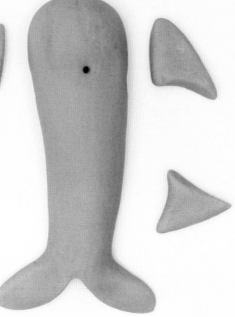

1 Shape the body, head and tail from 3 oz (84 g) gray paste. Roll into a tapered sausage, the head end being fatter than the tail end. Slice approximately 1 in (2.5 cm) through the tail using the X-acto knife. Shape the tail with your fingers and flatten the flippers slightly. Use the paper towel to support the tail until dry. Mark the blow hole with the pointed end of the flower veining tool.

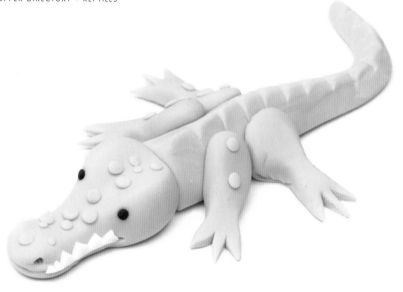

alligator

Not an aggressive alligator, just a friendly one.

Materials

- Modeling paste
- Corn starch
- Dry spaghetti
- Edible glue

Tools

- Workboard
- Small palette knife
- X-acto knife
- Flower veining tool

Colors Used

2¾ oz (77 g) lime green
⅛ oz (4 g) white
● Pinch black

Length: 5 in (12.5 cm)

See also
Pastes, icings, glues, pages 28–33 > Modeling techniques, pages 42–47 > Designing your figures, pages 48–51

3 For the head, shape ½ oz (14 g) lime green paste into a sausage, narrow the middle section and flatten one end for the snout. Mark the eye sockets, drawing the flower veining tool between them to accentuate. Mark the nose with the pointed end of the flower veining tool. Attach the head to the body using dry spaghetti and edible glue.

4 Cut the teeth from the white paste. Roll the paste thinly, then use the X-acto knife to cut two rows of teeth. Attach to either side of the face using edible glue.

5 Add two black eyes to the head, rolling the black paste into two balls and attaching to the head using edible glue.

2 For the front and back legs, shape 1 oz (28 g) lime green paste into four equal sausages. Make the back legs slightly fatter and shorter than the front ones. Pinch the middle of each leg in slightly, then flatten one end for the foot. Use the X-acto knife to cut out two triangles, leaving three toes. Attach to the body.

1 Make the body and tail of the alligator using 1 oz (28 g) lime green paste. Shape into a sausage, then pinch the top to make a ridge. Smooth any fingermarks away. Use the small palette knife to slice lines into the ridge to make spines. Curve the tail into position.

6 Make scales using the final remnants of green paste. Roll into balls, then flatten and attach to the face and legs using edible glue.

81 chameleon

Chameleons are full of character and, in fondant modeling, are made up of lots of interesting shapes.

Materials
- Modeling paste
- Corn starch
- Edible glue
- Medium-green petal dust

Tools
- Workboard
- Rolling pin
- Flower veining tool
- X-acto knife
- Dusting brush

Colors Used
- 4 oz (112 g) green
- Pinch black

Length: 6 in (15 cm)

See also
Pastes, icings, glues, pages 28–33 > Color mixing, pages 38–39 > Modeling techniques, pages 42–47

3 Shape two eyes from ⅛ oz (4 g) green paste. Roll into two balls and attach to the head using edible glue.

4 Attach two balls of black paste to the eyes with edible glue for the pupils.

2 Make the head using ¾ oz (21 g) green paste. Shape into an egg shape, but raise up the broader end where it will join the body. Flatten down the head toward the nose area. Mark the mouth with the X-acto knife.

1 Roll 2⅛ oz (60 g) of green paste into a long sausage, thinner at one end than the other. Curl the thinner end around into a coil. Shape the back of the chameleon so that it is raised slightly, and use the flower veining tool to indent this raised area: begin with only a slight indentation at the tail end but, as you work further up the back toward the head end, make the indentations deeper and more pronounced.

5 Shape each leg from ⅛ oz (4 g) green paste. Roll each into a short sausage, flatten slightly, then cut one triangle out of the end to shape into the two toes of the chameleon. Bend the front legs at the elbow section. Attach the legs to the body using edible glue.

6 Dust the chameleon with medium-green petal dust to add depth to the shape.

82 bullfrog

A cheerful frog!

Materials

- Modeling paste
- Corn starch
- Edible glue
- Green petal dust

Tools

- Workboard
- Rolling pin
- Small palette knife
- Bone tool
- Flower veining tool
- X-acto knife
- Dusting brush

Colors Used

- 4½ oz (126 g) light green
- Pinch red
- Pinch black

Length: 3½ in (9 cm)

See also
Color mixing, pages 38–39 > Modeling techniques, pages 42–47 > Props, pages 248–253

EASY

4 Make two eyes with the red paste and secure with edible glue. Add a black ball to finish each eye. Secure in place in the same way.

5 Make the front legs from ½ oz (14 g) green paste. Shape into two teardrops but without the point. Flatten the narrow end for the front feet. Shape the front feet using the X-acto knife. Bend at a 90-degree angle. Attach the front legs to the body using edible glue.

6 Dust the frog with green petal dust to add depth.

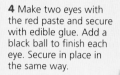

3 Shape the feet from ½ oz (14 g) green paste. Roll into two egg shapes, then flatten. Cut the toes with the X-acto knife and use the flower veining tool to score the feet. Tuck the feet under the ends of the legs and secure in place using edible glue.

2 Shape the back legs from 1½ oz (42 g) green paste. Roll into two equal sausages, one end longer than the other. Bend over, not quite in half, tucking part of the fatter end under the abdomen of the frog. Secure in place using edible glue. Tuck the legs up neatly near the body, securing in place with edible glue.

1 Make the body from 2 oz (56 g) green paste. Roll into a teardrop shape, flattening and softening the point to the teardrop. Use the small palette knife to mark the mouth of the frog. Indent the eye sockets with the smaller end of the bone tool, and run a groove between the eyes with the flat end of the flower veining tool to accentuate the eyes. Follow the groove down the body of the frog, and accentuate the ridges either side of the groove at the base of the body.

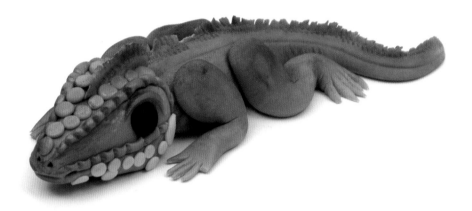

83 lizard

A shy little lizard, minding his own business.

Materials

- Modeling paste
- Corn starch
- Edible glue
- Mid-green petal dust
- Brown petal dust

Tools

- Workboard
- Rolling pin
- Scissors
- Small palette knife
- Flower veining tool
- Ball tool
- X-acto knife
- Dusting brush

Colors Used

- ● 5¼ oz (147 g) green
- ● Pinch black
- Pinch cream

Length: 6 in (15 cm)

See also
Pastes, icings, glues, pages 28–33 > Color mixing, pages 38–39 > Modeling techniques, pages 42–47

3 Make the ridges for the head using six strands of green paste. Roll into long sausages, and use the flower veining tool to indent all the way along each one. Attach to the face with edible glue, on each side, one from the nostrils over the head to behind the eyes, one running around the eye, and one along the jaw line.

4 For the spots, take tiny pinches of green and cream paste, roll into balls, flatten, and attach to the face and head using edible glue.

2 For the head, shape 1 oz (28 g) green paste into a triangle, softening the edges. Mark the mouth with the small palette knife and the nostrils with the pointed end of the flower veining tool. Use the ball tool to indent the eye sockets. Roll two pinches of black paste into balls for the eyes, and secure with edible glue.

5 Make the front legs by shaping ½ oz (14 g) green paste into two teardrops, keeping the broad end big. Bend the narrower end forward for the front leg. Make the webbed feet using the X-acto knife. Attach to the front of the body using edible glue.

6 For the back legs, shape 1½ oz (42 g) green paste into two long teardrops with a large broad end, lengthen the teardrop, and flatten the narrower end. Cut the toes from the flatter end using the X-acto knife. Bend the leg at the knee, then bend it back on itself for the foot. Attach to the back of the body with edible glue.

1 For the body and tail, shape 2 oz (56 g) green paste into a long, graduating sausage, narrower at one end for the tail. Pinch a ridge along the top of the body, thin this out, and then snip it with scissors to make spines. Draw the pointed end of the scissors down each side of the body to texture the paste.

7 Dust the lizard with mid-green and brown petal dusts.

EASY

84 snake

This slithery character is ready to attack!

To create the stripy effect here, don't blend all the paste when coloring (see page 38).

1 Shape the snake from the whole amount of green paste.

2 Roll the paste into a long sausage that is slightly fatter at one end. At the fatter end, roll the rolling pin over each side of the sausage, without flattening the center of the shape.

3 Flatten the side sections as much as you can. Use the flower veining tool to add texture lines across the whole of the snake.

4 Use the flower veining tool to mark the mouth.

5 Stand the snake up and support using paper towels to support until dry.

6 Shape the tongue from the pink paste. Roll into a sausage, flatten one end, cut a "V" shape in the flattened end using the X-acto knife, insert dry spaghetti into the tongue to support, and attach to the snake's mouth with edible glue.

7 Make the eyes by rolling the black paste into two balls. Attach with edible glue.

8 Dust the snake with light-green petal dust to add depth.

Materials
- Modeling paste
- Corn starch
- Edible glue
- Dry spaghetti
- Light green petal dust

Tools
- Workboard
- Rolling pin
- Flower veining tool
- Paper towel
- X-acto knife
- Dusting brush

Colors Used
- 2 oz (56 g) green
- Pinch pink
- Pinch black

Length: 5½ in (14 cm)

See also
Pastes, icings, glues, pages 28–33 > Color mixing, pages 38–39 > Modeling techniques, pages 42–47

snail

This simple model can be made in any color to go with your cake design.

1 For the body, shape the pale pink paste so that one end is thicker than the other. Flatten this end with your thumb, then, on the longer side, mark the mouth with the small palette knife. Curl the body slightly up at the head. Support with paper towel until dry.

2 Shape two small pink balls from ⅛ oz (4 g) medium-pink paste for the eyes. Dust the wire with the pink petal dust, curl, then insert into the head. Attach the eyes to the end of the wire, paint white eyeballs onto the eyes with the edible white paint, and add pupils made from two tiny pinches of black paste.

3 Roll the dark pink paste into a tapered sausage. Start coiling up from the thinnest end, allowing it to protrude slightly as you roll. Attach to the body section using edible glue.

4 Finish off with the shell cover, using the rest of the medium-pink paste. Shape into a sausage, taper at both ends and attach to the body with edible glue, between the body and the shell.

Materials
- Modeling paste
- Corn starch
- Edible glue
- Pink petal dust
- Edible white paint
- Two 2-in (5-cm) lengths 24 ga. wire

Tools
- Workboard
- Rolling pin
- Small palette knife
- Paper towel
- Dusting brush
- Paint brush

Colors Used
- ● 1 oz (28 g) pale pink
- ● 1 oz (28 g) dark pink
- ● ¼ oz (7 g) medium pink
- ● Pinch black

Length: 5½ in (14 cm)

See also
Color mixing, pages 38–39 > Modeling techniques, pages 42–47 > Designing your figures, pages 48–51

ant

This inquisitive ant looks good large and on his own, or make him smaller and give him some companions.

Materials

- Modeling paste
- Corn starch
- Dry spaghetti
- Edible glue
- Edible black paint
- Three 6-in (15-cm) lengths 26 ga. wire

Tools

- Workboard
- Rolling pin
- Flower veining tool
- Paint brush

Colors Used

● 1 oz (28 g) black
○ Pinch white

Length: 3½ in (9 cm)

See also
Pastes, icings, glues, pages 28–33 > Modeling techniques, pages 42–47 > Designing your figures, pages 48–51

6 Paint the wires with edible black paint and leave to dry.

7 Cut two 6-in (15-cm) lengths of 26 ga. wire into three equal lengths. Bend each wire three times to create a zigzag. Insert the wires into the thorax to give your ant legs.

5 For the antennae, cut a 6-in (15-cm) length of 26 ga. wire in half. Wind each wire around a paint brush or flower veining tool to coil it up. Insert the wires into the head.

8 Create eyes from two tiny pinches of white paste topped with two tiny pinches of black paste. Secure in place with edible glue.

4 Shape the head section into a teardrop using ⅛ oz (4 g) black paste. Attach as before.

3 Shape the thorax into an egg shape, using less than ⅛ oz (4 g) black paste. Attach to the abdomen sections with edible glue and dry spaghetti.

2 Roll two tiny balls from two pinches of black paste. Attach to the narrow end of the abdomen, pushing down the dry spaghetti. Use edible glue between each segment, if needed.

1 Shape the abdomen from ½ oz (14 g) black paste. Roll into an elongated egg shape, and narrow the pointed end. Push dry spaghetti into the end to assist the join.

dragonfly

The blue hair, large eyes and triangular nose give this dragonfly lots of character.

Materials

- Gum paste
- Modeling paste
- Corn starch
- Edible glue
- Dry spaghetti
- Three 6-in (15-cm) lengths blue 26 ga. wire

Tools

- Workboard
- Rolling pin
- Pizza cutter
- X-acto knife
- Small palette knife

Colors Used

- ¾ oz (21 g) lime green
- ¾ oz (21 g) bright blue
- ½ oz (14 g) white gum paste
- Pinch black
- Pinch white

Length: 5 in (12 cm)

See also
Pastes, icings, glues, pages 28–33 > Modeling techniques, pages 42–47 > Designing your figures, pages 48–51

5 Add a nose to the face using a pinch of lime green paste rolled and shaped into a pyramid. Attach as before.

6 Shape the legs from a 6-in (15-cm) length of wire. Cut into four equal pieces, bend, and insert the longest section into the body of the dragonfly.

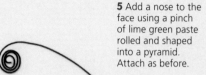

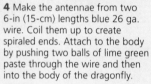

4 Make the antennae from two 6-in (15-cm) lengths blue 26 ga. wire. Coil them up to create spiraled ends. Attach to the body by pushing two balls of lime green paste through the wire and then into the body of the dragonfly.

7 For the tail, roll ¾ oz (21 g) blue paste into a sausage, tapering one end. Score the tail with the small palette knife. Cut the broader end flat. Insert dry spaghetti into the tail, dab with edible glue, and attach to the body. Support the tail in an upward position until dry.

3 Add two eyes by rolling the white paste into two balls. Flatten, attach together, and then attach to the top of the body. Add two tiny flattened balls of black paste in the same way. Roll two pinches of lime green paste into two bananas and attach above the eyes for eyebrows.

2 For the body, roll ½ oz (14 g) lime green paste into a sausage, leaving one end curved. Cut the other end flat with the X-acto knife. Indent the mouth with the small palette knife.

8 Use the remnants of the blue paste to make hair by rolling it flat and cutting tufts with the X-acto knife. Secure with edible glue.

1 To make the wings, roll out the gum paste quite thinly. Using the pizza cutter, cut out four elongated oval wings. Leave to dry thoroughly on a flat surface.

9 Attach the wings to the dragonfly using edible glue.

bumblebee

A really cute insect that is lots of fun to make. Remember to tell the recipient of this topper that the antennae are non-edible.

Materials

- Gum paste
- Modeling paste
- Corn starch
- Edible glue
- Dry spaghetti
- Two 6-in (15-cm) lengths gold floral wire
- Six 2-in (5-cm) lengths 26 ga. wire
- Yellow floral tape
- Black petal dust
- Royal icing

Tools

- Workboard
- Rolling pin
- Fondant impression mat (optional)
- X-acto knife
- Flower veining tool
- Paint brush

Colors Used

- 1½ oz (42 g) yellow
- 1⅛ oz (32 g) black
- 1 oz (28 g) white gum paste
- ⅛ oz (4 g) white

Length: 3 in (8 cm)

See also
Pastes, icings, glues, pages 28–33 > Modeling techniques, pages 42–47 > Designing your figures, pages 48–51

5 Roll two further tiny balls of black paste, flatten slightly, and attach to the head. Coil the two gold wires around the handle of a paint brush for the antennae. Insert each one into the black balls on the head.

4 Make the eyeballs from the white paste. Shape into two tiny egg shapes and attach to the head using edible glue. Add two eyeballs using two tiny balls of black paste.

6 Make the legs from the 2-in (5-cm) lengths 26 ga. wire. Tape the wire using yellow floral tape. Bend the wire as shown. Insert into the body. Dust with black petal dust.

3 Shape the head from ¼ oz (7 g) black paste. Roll into a ball and attach to the body with edible glue and dry spaghetti.

2 Shape the body next. Make the large yellow segment first using 1 oz (28 g) yellow modeling paste. Roll into a ball and flatten slightly. Use the flower veining tool to score the paste. Next, make the black segment in the same way from ¾ oz (21 g) black paste, and butt it up against the larger yellow shape. Make the second yellow segment in the same way, using ½ oz (14 g) paste.

7 Attach the wings to the bee just above the legs, using dabs of royal icing.

1 To make the wings, roll out the white gum paste thinly. If you want, you can texture the wings using a fondant impression mat. Use the X-acto knife to cut out four elongated triangles and leave to dry flat.

pink butterfly

This butterfly is created using brush embroidery, which is a method of painting with colored royal icing.

Materials

- Gum paste
- Modeling paste
- Corn starch
- 2 oz (56 g) royal icing
- Piping gel
- Two 3-in (7.5-cm) lengths pink 26 ga. wire
- Silver petal dust or edible luster spray

Tools

- Workboard
- Rolling pin
- Butterfly cutter
- Cardboard
- Piping bag
- Decorating tip No. 3
- Paint brush
- Flower veining tool
- Dusting brush

Colors Used

- 1 oz (28 g) pink or black gum paste
- 1 oz (28 g) pink

Length: 3½ in (9 cm)

See also
Pastes, icings, glues, pages 28–33 > Color mixing, pages 38–39 > Designing a cake, pages 52–53

4 Make the body and head of the butterfly from 1 oz (28 g) pink paste. Shape into a tapered sausage, marking indentations along the body if you wish with the flower veining tool. Mark the head. Attach to the wings with dots of royal icing.

3 Pipe short lines of royal icing on the butterfly, starting on the edge of the wings, working inward the whole time. Spread the damp bristles of a paint brush and draw it lightly over the line of piping. You need to work fairly quickly. Continue through the wing, changing color as you go. Leave to dry.

5 Insert the 26 ga. wire into the head for two pink antennae, either prepared as for the dragonfly (see page 221, step 4) or coiled (wrap the wire around your pinky).

6 Lightly dust the finished butterfly with a little silver petal dust to add sparkle, or use an edible luster spray.

2 Color the royal icing (see pages 38–39). Add a little piping gel to each color, then load the piping bag with the decorating tip and add the royal icing.

1 Roll out the pink (or black) gum paste and cut out a butterfly shape using the butterfly cutter. Place on a piece of creased cardboard to hold the butterfly in a slightly bent position.

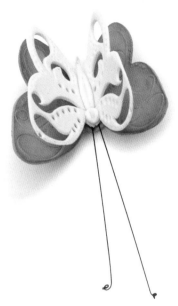

blue butterfly

Make more than one butterfly to create a flock of butterflies fluttering on your cake. The antennae are not edible.

Materials

- Gum paste
- Corn starch
- Edible glue
- Blue petal dust
- Royal icing
- Two 3-in (7.5-cm) lengths 24 ga. blue metallic wire

Tools

- Workboard
- Rolling pin
- Butterfly cutter (or butterfly template and X-acto knife)
- Drying former (or very thick cardboard)
- Dusting brush
- Various cutters
- Decorating tip No. 2
- X-acto knife
- Paper towel

Colors Used

- ½ oz (14 g) blue gum paste
- ½ oz (14 g) white gum paste

Length: 3½ in (9 cm)

See also

Pastes, icings, glues, pages 28–33 > Modeling techniques, pages 42–47 > Designing a cake, pages 52–53

5 Place the lacy wings over the butterfly shape. Support on rolled-up paper towel at the edges, allowing the cut center to sit in the center of the butterfly. Secure in place with royal icing.

6 Shape an elongated teardrop body from the remnants of white gum paste and place in the center of the butterfly over the top of the royal icing. Make the head by rolling a pinch of white gum paste into a ball and attach to the body with edible glue.

4 Cut out the same butterfly shape from the white gum paste, but in a slightly smaller size. Use a selection of cutters to create a lacy effect on the wings. Indent the wings with the end of the decorating tip to create tiny dots. Cut the butterfly in half with the X-acto knife and dry flat. Dust lightly, if you wish, when dry.

7 Insert two strands of metallic blue wire into the head of the butterfly for the antennae.

3 When the butterfly is dry, dust the edges with a deeper shade of blue petal dust to accentuate the outer shape.

2 Place the butterfly shape in the drying former. If you don't have a drying former, use a piece of cardboard bent in half to the correct angle to support the butterfly.

1 Roll out the blue gum paste thinly with the rolling pin. Cut out the butterfly either with a cutter, which is the easiest way, or by using a template and an X-acto knife.

91 ladybug

Ladybugs are considered lucky in many cultures, so top off a good luck cake with this colorful creature.

Materials

- Modeling paste
- Corn starch
- Edible glue
- Two 3½-in (9-cm) lengths 24 ga. wire
- Yellow petal dust

Tools

- Workboard
- Rolling pin
- X-acto knife
- Flower veining tool
- Bone tool
- Scallop tool
- Dusting brush
- Decorating tip No. 1

Colors Used

- ● 1⅓ oz (37 g) red
- ○ ⅞ oz (25 g) yellow
- ● ⅛ oz (4 g) black
- ○ Pinch white

Length: 2¾ in (7 cm)

See also
Pastes, icings, glues, pages 28–33 > Modeling techniques, pages 42–47 > Designing your figures, pages 48–51

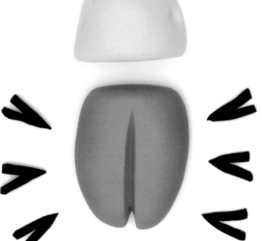

4 Make the eyes from ¼ oz (7 g) yellow paste. Roll into a ball and cut in half to create two semicircles. Attach to the head using edible glue. Finish the eyes with pinches of white for the eyeballs and black for the pupils.

5 For the antennae, dust the wire with yellow petal dust, then push into the head of the ladybird. Attach a pinch of yellow paste to the end of each wire.

3 Roll a pinch of yellow paste into a ball for a nose, and attach with edible glue.

2 Use ⅝ oz (18 g) yellow paste to make the head. Roll into a ball, flatten on one side, then cut off a small section to line up with the body. Use the flower veining tool to mark the mouth, and the bone tool to mark the dimples. Use the scallop tool to mark the ends of the smile.

6 Roll out half the black paste and cut out the spots using the decorating tip. Secure in place with edible glue.

1 Shape all the red paste into an oval and cut off a little from one end using the X-acto knife, leaving a flat end. Flatten the base. Use the flower veining tool to make an indentation up the center of the body to shape the wings. Make the indentation deep at the pointed end, then shallower as you draw it up.

7 With the remaining black paste and the X-acto knife, cut out the feet. Cut out a long triangle, then cut out the center of it, leaving two legs. Attach under each side of the body with edible glue.

92 spider

This is an angry little spider, but you can change his facial expression easily by molding the lips and eyes differently.

Materials

- Modeling paste
- Corn starch
- Edible glue
- Eight 2-in (5-cm) lengths of 22 ga. wire

Tools

- Workboard
- Rolling pin
- Wire cutter
- Flower veining tool

Colors Used

- ● 3½ oz (98 g) black
- ○ Pinch white

Height: 2 in (5 cm)

See also
Pastes, icings, glues, pages 28–33 > Modeling techniques, pages 42–47 > Designing your figures, pages 48–51

3 As you insert the wire into the body, add a tiny ball of paste, made from an additional pinch of black paste. Secure with edible glue.

4 Make the eyes from the white paste. Roll into a ball, flatten, and cut in half. Attach with edible glue. Shape the pupil using a pinch of black paste and secure in the same way. Shape two eyebrows from two pinches of black paste rolled into sausages. Secure in place with edible glue.

5 Shape a mouth from ⅛ oz (4 g) black paste. Draw the flower veining tool through the middle to separate the lips, then secure in place using edible glue.

1 Shape 2 oz (56 g) black paste into a round ball to form the spider's body.

2 The legs are all made in the same way. Use 1 oz (28 g) black paste to make all eight legs. Shape into eight teardrops and insert a wire into each one. Smooth the paste over the wire, leaving a tiny part of the wire exposed to insert into the body.

93 scorpion

A fearsome arachnid, even when made from modeling paste.

Materials

- Modeling paste
- Corn starch
- Dry spaghetti
- Edible glue
- Eight 2-in (5-cm) lengths and one 8-in (20-cm) length 26 ga. wire

Tools

- Workboard
- Rolling pin
- Flower veining tool
- X-acto knife
- Wire cutter

Colors Used

- 6¼ oz (175 g) red
- ⅛ oz (4 g) white
- Pinch black

Length: 6 in (15 cm)

See also
Pastes, icings, glues, pages 28–33 > Modeling techniques, pages 42–47 > Designing your figures, pages 48–51

3 To make the two front pincers, shape ½ oz (14 g) red paste into two ovals oval, flatten slightly, and divide the two pincers using the X-acto knife. Indent the inside of the cut with the flower veining tool to give a serrated appearance. Attach to the arms using edible glue.

4 Shape a pinch of red paste into a cigar shape. Curve slightly and attach to the front of the body for the mouth of the scorpion. Score with the flower veining tool to texture.

2 Make four cones from 1 oz (28 g) red paste for the arms. Attach the components together using dry spaghetti. Attach to the body using dry spaghetti and a dab of edible glue.

5 Roll two pinches of white paste into balls. Attach to the scorpion above the mouth for two eyeballs. Add the pupils in the same way.

1 Shape 1 oz (28 g) red paste into an oval, then score the surface with the flower veining tool to create a segmented appearance.

6 The eight legs are made in the same way. Bend a 2-in (5-cm) length 26 ga. wire into three equal sections. Use ¼ oz (7 g) red paste and push two teardrops onto two sections of the wire, leaving the third section free (this is inserted into the body). Secure the legs in place with edible glue before pushing the wire into the body.

7 For the tail, make five cones from 1½ oz (42 g) red paste. Thread these onto an 8-in (20-cm) length 26 ga. wire, securing each with a dot of edible glue. Bend the wire forward over the body of the scorpion and push the end into the tail end of the body.

94 woolly mammoth

The defining characteristics of this woolly mammoth are his coat and his enormous tusks, both of which are very easy to make.

Materials

- Modeling paste
- Corn starch
- Dry spaghetti
- Edible glue
- Brown petal dust
- Black petal dust

Tools

- Workboard
- Rolling pin
- Scallop tool
- Pizza cutter
- Flower veining tool
- Small palette knife
- Bone tool
- Paper towel
- Dusting brush

Colors Used

- 8¼ oz (231 g) gray
- 1 oz (28 g) cream
- Pinch black

Height: 5½ in (14 cm)

See also
Pastes, icings, glues, pages 28–33 > Color mixing, pages 38–39 > Modeling techniques, pages 42–47

5 Shape the ears from 1½ oz (42 g) gray paste. Roll into two balls, then flatten with the rolling pin. Score the ends of the ears with the pizza cutter and the flower veining tool. Attach to the head using edible glue.

6 For the hair, roll out ¼ oz (7 g) gray paste and score as before. Attach to the head using edible glue.

4 For the head, roll 2 oz (56 g) gray paste into an elongated teardrop. Score along the length of the trunk using the small palette knife. Add two indentations for the tusks using the bone tool, and mark the eyes with the end of the flower veining tool. Attach to the body using edible glue and dry spaghetti. Bend the trunk and support in place until dry using paper towel. Add two tiny eyes using pinches of black paste.

7 For the tusks, roll the cream paste into two sausages and thin one end. Attach the fatter end to the head of the mammoth using edible glue and dry spaghetti. Support the ends of the tusk so they dry in the curved position.

8 Dust the tusks with brown petal dust. Dust the tips of the "fur" with black petal dust.

3 Roll out 1 oz (28 g) gray paste. Score the paste with the pizza cutter and the flower veining tool. Drape over the body to create a woolly look for your mammoth.

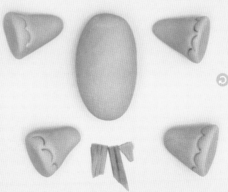

1 For the feet, roll 1½ oz (42 g) gray paste into four cones and mark the toes with the scallop tool. Push dry spaghetti through each foot.

2 For the body, roll 2 oz (56 g) gray paste into an oval ball and attach on top of the feet and dry spaghetti, using edible glue to secure.

95 spinosaurus

Have fun dusting your spinosaurus with green and yellow petal dust.

Materials

- Modeling paste
- Corn starch
- Edible glue
- Dry spaghetti
- Green petal dust
- Yellow petal dust

Tools

- Workboard
- Rolling pin
- X-acto knife
- Flower veining tool
- Ball tool
- Decorating tip No. 1
- Dusting brush

Colors Used

- 6½ oz (182 g) cream
- Pinch black

Length: 6½ in (16 cm)

See also
Pastes, icings, glues, pages 28–33 > Color mixing, pages 38–39 > Modeling techniques, pages 42–47

5 Insert two black balls of paste for the eyes. Use edible glue to secure in place.

4 Shape 1 oz (28 g) cream paste into an elongated teardrop, flattening the narrow end, for the head. Score the mouth using the flower veining tool. Indent the nostrils and eye sockets with the small end of the ball tool. Attach the head to the top of the body with edible glue and dry spaghetti.

6 Shape the spines from 1 oz (28 g) cream paste. Flatten into a semicircle shape and, using the big end of the decorating tip, cut out the edge leaving a scalloped shape. Texture down the spines using the flower veining tool and attach to the back.

3 Shape the front legs from ½ oz (14 g) cream paste. Roll two teardrop shapes and create the front claws as before, securing to the top of the body with edible glue.

2 Roll 1 oz (28 g) cream paste into an elongated teardrop for the back legs. Bend at the knee and ankle, flattening the foot section. Use the X-acto knife to cut out two triangles from the foot to leave three toes. Attach to either side of the abdomen with edible glue.

1 Roll 3 oz (84 g) cream paste into a sausage, elongating the tail and leaving the body section fatter so that the body will stand up.

7 Dust the spinosaurus with green and yellow petal dust.

96 saber-tooth tiger

Those teeth look ferocious, but this saber-tooth tiger won't hurt you!

Materials

- Modeling paste
- Corn starch
- Edible glue
- Dry spaghetti
- Shortening

Tools

- Workboard
- Rolling pin
- Flower veining tool
- Ball tool
- Clay gun with multihole disk

Colors Used

- 3¾ oz (105 g) orange
- ⅝ oz (18 g) white
- ½ oz (14 g) black

Length: 4 in (10 cm)

See also
Pastes, icings, glues, pages 28–33 > Modeling techniques, pages 42–47 > Designing your figures, pages 48–51

4 Use ⅛ oz (4 g) orange paste for the ears. Shape into two teardrops, indent the centers, and attach to the head with edible glue.

5 Roll two pinches of white paste into balls for the eyes, and secure in place with edible glue. Add in two black pupils, securing as before.

6 Shape the muzzle from ⅛ oz (4 g) white paste. Roll two balls, flatten, and attach to the face with edible glue. Add a pinch of white paste for the mouth. Attach as before. Add a black nose made from a pinch of black paste.

3 Shape 1 oz (28 g) orange paste into a triangle, pulling out the side points slightly. Flatten and texture using the flower veining tool. Indent the eye sockets using the smaller end of the ball tool. Attach two pinches of white paste to the side of the face as facial fur, and texture as before.

7 For the tusks, roll ⅛ oz (4 g) white paste into two elongated cones. Insert dry spaghetti into the fatter end, and attach to the face using edible glue.

8 Add shortening to the remaining black paste to make it soft, then extrude the paste through the clay gun with a multihole disk and attach to the head and back using edible glue.

2 Shape ¼ oz (7 g) orange paste into two sausages with narrower middles. Indent the paws with the flower veining tool and attach to the front of the body with edible glue. Allow the paws to stick out in front of the body. The back legs are shaped from ⅛ oz (4 g) orange paste. Roll into two teardrops, texture the paws as before, and attach to the body next to the indentations for the back legs.

1 Shape 2 oz (56 g) orange paste into a teardrop. Flatten slightly at the head end, and indent either side of the shape for the back legs.

9 Roll ⅛ oz (4 g) orange paste into a teardrop for the tail. Texture using the flower veining tool and attach with edible glue.

97 brachiosaurus

Balancing the long neck of the brachiosaurus is rather challenging, but the results are worth it.

Materials
- Modeling paste
- Corn starch
- Dry spaghetti
- Edible glue
- 6-in (15-cm) length 22 ga. wire
- Shortening

Tools
- Workboard
- Rolling pin
- Scallop tool
- Flower veining tool
- Clay gun with multihole disk

Colors Used
- 4½ oz (126 g) green
- ¼ oz (7 g) white
- Pinch black

Height: 6½ in (16 cm)

See also
Pastes, icings, glues, pages 28–33 > Modeling techniques, pages 42–47 > Props, pages 248–253

4 Shape the white paste into two balls and attach to the head using edible glue for eyes. Add two tiny balls of black paste for pupils, and secure with edible glue as before.

5 Roll pinches of green paste into two teardrops and score down the middle using the flower veining tool. Attach ears to the head using edible glue.

6 Make the hair by blending shortening with a pinch of green paste. Place in the clay gun and extrude through the multihole disk. Attach to the head, neck and back of the brachiosaurus, securing in place with edible glue.

3 For the neck, shape ½ oz (14 g) of green paste into a long sausage and thread a 6-in (15-cm) 22 ga. wire through it, leaving a section to insert into the body. Smooth and even out. Insert the wire into the body and secure in place with edible glue. Shape the head from another ½ oz (14 g) green paste and attach to the top of the neck using edible glue. Indent the nostrils using the flower veining tool. Support until dry.

1 Roll 1 oz (28 g) green paste into four cones for the feet. Mark the toes with the scallop tool and leave to dry.

2 Shape 2 oz (56 g) green paste into an elongated teardrop for the body. Lengthen out the tail and coil around the body. Attach to the feet using dry spaghetti and edible glue.

triceratops

The gleam in this triceratops' eye really brings him to life.

Materials

- Modeling paste
- Corn starch
- Edible glue
- Dry spaghetti
- Edible white paint

Tools

- Workboard
- Rolling pin
- Scallop tool
- Flower veining tool
- Ball tool
- Paint brush

Colors Used

- 4¾ oz (133 g) dark green
- ¼ oz (7 g) light green
- ¼ oz (7 g) ivory
- Pinch white
- Pinch black

Length: 4 in (10 cm)

See also
Pastes, icings, glues, pages 28–33 > Modeling techniques, pages 42–47 > Designing your figures, pages 48–51

5 Shape two large horns and one short horn from the ivory paste. Attach to the head using dry spaghetti and edible glue. The smallest one goes on top of the nose; the larger ones go on the forehead.

4 Shape 1 oz (28 g) dark green paste into an egg shape. Narrow the sides a little and pull the nose end out a little. Shape the mouth with the flower veining tool, and pull the upper lip out a little. Indent the eye sockets with the small end of the ball tool. Attach to the body using edible glue and dry spaghetti.

3 Shape ½ oz (14 g) dark green paste into a rough disk for the neck armor. Indent with the flower veining tool to give a scalloped edge and use the flat end of the flower veining tool to texture the disk. Attach to the neck using edible glue.

2 For the front legs, roll ½ oz (14 g) dark green paste into two cones. Use the scallop tool to indent the toes. Bend over at the ankle section and attach to the body near the head end. Shape the back legs from ¾ oz (21 g) dark green paste. Bend twice to give a knee and ankle. Flatten against the back of the body with edible glue. Mark the toes as before.

6 Add two white balls to the eye sockets followed by two black pupils, secured with edible glue. Paint a white dot onto the pupils with edible white paint.

7 For the scales, take pinches of light green paste, roll into a ball and flatten, securing in place with edible glue.

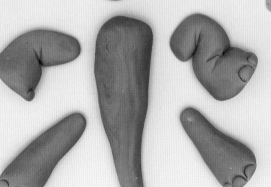

1 Shape the body from 2 oz (56 g) dark green paste. Roll into a sausage, narrowing out one end.

99 tyrannosaurus rex

A quirky-looking Tyrannosaurus Rex for a dinosaur-themed cake.

Materials

- Modeling paste
- Corn starch
- Edible glue
- Dry spaghetti
- Shortening
- Edible white paint
- Pink petal dust

Tools

- Workboard
- Rolling pin
- Flower veining tool
- Ball tool
- Small palette knife
- Paper towel
- Clay gun with multihole disk
- Paint brush
- X-acto knife
- Dusting brush

Colors Used

- 4½ oz (126 g) light green
- 1 oz (28 g) dark green
- ¾ oz (21 g) white
- ½ oz (14 g) yellow
- Pinch black

Height: 6 in (15 cm)

See also
Pastes, icings, glues, pages 28–33 > Color mixing, pages 38–39 > Modeling techniques, pages 42–47

5 Shape 1 oz (28 g) light green paste into an egg shape for the head. Attach to the body, with the narrower end toward the back, using edible glue and dry spaghetti. Indent the eye sockets using the small end of the ball tool. Mark and cut the mouth using the small palette knife. Insert a tiny roll of paper towel into the mouth to support. Mark the nostrils with the pointed end of the flower veining tool.

6 Take ½ oz (14 g) dark green paste, add some shortening to it to soften, and extrude in the clay gun with the multihole disk to create strands of hair. Attach to the head with edible glue.

4 Shape the forearms from ½ oz (14 g) light green paste. Roll into two sausages, flatten one end, and cut two triangles from the end, leaving three claws. Attach to the top of the body using edible glue.

7 Roll ¼ oz (14 g) white paste into two balls for the eyes and attach to the head using edible glue. Add two black pupils, securing as before. Paint a tiny white dot on each pupil with edible white paint.

3 Shape the yellow paste into an oval. Flatten one side and mark lines across the paste using the flower veining tool. Attach to the front of the body using edible glue.

8 Roll out the remaining white paste thinly. Cut out triangles using the X-acto knife to create a row of sharp teeth. Attach to the mouth with edible glue.

2 Shape the rear legs into teardrops using 1 oz (28 g) light green paste. Flatten the narrow end and cut three tiny triangles out of the end to create four toes. Bend the foot up and attach to the side of the body, securing with edible glue.

9 Add triangular spines down the back using the remaining dark green paste. Secure in place with edible glue.

1 Shape 2 oz (56 g) light green paste into a teardrop, then elongate the thinner end while pulling the fatter end into a tail. Keep the middle section fatter. Stand up with the tail out behind the shape, keeping it upright.

10 Dust the cheeks with pink petal dust.

100 stegosaurus

You can make this herbivore dinosaur in any color you choose.

Materials

- Modeling paste
- Corn starch
- Dry spaghetti
- Edible glue

Tools

- Workboard
- Rolling pin
- Scallop tool
- Flower veining tool
- Round cutters, large and small
- X-acto knife

Colors Used

- 4⅛ oz (116 g) yellow
- 1½ oz (42 g) green
- Pinch black
- Pinch white

Length: 3½ in (9 cm)

See also
Pastes, icings, glues, pages 28–33 > Modeling techniques, pages 42–47 > Designing your figures, pages 48–51

3 Roll the white paste into two balls for eyes. Attach to the head using edible glue, and add in two black pupils. Roll two pinches of yellow paste into sausages for brows. Attach above the eyes and add texturing with the flower veining tool.

2 Roll 2 oz (56 g) yellow paste into a sausage that is fatter in the middle. Attach to the feet by pushing each foot onto the underside of the body. Use edible glue to secure in place. Allow the head to be lower than the tail.

1 Make four feet from 2 oz (56 g) yellow paste. Roll into four cones and indent the toes using the scallop tool. Push dry spaghetti into the top of each one. Allow to dry.

5 For the scales, take pinches of the remaining green paste, roll into a ball, and flatten. Attach to the dinosaur with edible glue.

4 For the armor plating, roll out 1 oz (28 g) green paste and cut four large and four small circles with the cutters. Cut off one end with the X-acto knife to give a flat base. Score each one with the flower veining tool and attach down the back of the stegosaurus with edible glue, the larger ones in the center; the smaller ones either end. Hold onto them for a few seconds and they will stay put.

props

Once you have made your topper and your cake, you need to set the scene to display your creations at their absolute best. These props are easy to make and are inspiring ideas to get you thinking of more.

Make the props from modeling paste or gum paste if they need some support. If you are worried that they might not stand up, you can use the same supports that you have used on your models. You can push food-grade sticks directly into your cake without the need for a flower spike. For even more support, lean the prop up against the side of the cake.

Bale of straw
Straw bales are perfect for a farmyard theme or zoo theme. Shape the paste into a rectangle and pinch the edges to sharpen. Score the length of the rectangle with a flower veining tool and small palette knife. Use the serrated end of a tracing tool on the ends to texture.

Leaves
This simple leaf is ideal for a jungle theme. Make a basic teardrop shape with the point cut off. Cut out the central veins with an X-acto knife. You could make several leaves of different colors and sizes and arrange them around the side of the cake to create a jungle for the gorilla on page 160.

Bushes
These bushes work in any setting. For a beach setting, change the shade of the paste to a sandy color. Roll the colored paste into a semicircle, wrap the paste around a texture mat, and press firmly.

Banana

Shape only the center of the banana from gum paste. This will set hard and make the banana skin easier to attach. Make each peel of skin separately by shaping thin, elliptical shapes and attach to the center with edible glue. Dust with a little brown petal dust or a few dots of brown paint.

Branch

This branch would work well in many settings—zoo, farmyard, or jungle. Use 24 ga. florist's wire, bent and shaped, and then cover it with brown fondant. Texture the paste with a flower veining tool and don't forget to tell the recipient that this contains wire.

Milk churn

A must for the farmyard. Shape the paste into a cylinder. Cut into sections and, with your fingers, narrow the top. Shape a lid and attach with edible glue. Cut the handles by slicing narrow sections, bend round and attach to the side of the churn.

Flower head

These can be made large to accommodate a fly or butterfly (see page 224), or really small for any theme including under the sea. Use a flower cutter and gum paste. Soften the edges of the petals on the foam pad using a bone tool, and lay in a curved former until firm.

Straw

Roll out the paste fairly thinly and, using a pizza cutter, cut strands of paste. Leave them to dry separately and bunch together when dry.

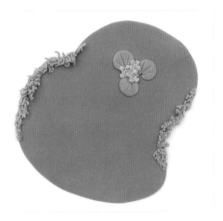

Pond

Roll out a piece of paste thinly, ideally into an unusual shape. Grass, flowers and lilypads can be added to create a more authentic appearance. Push green paste through a sieve and attach around the edge of the pond with edible glue.

Tree

Shape the trunk around a lollipop stick, making the top narrower and the base broad. Pinch the base to create the distinctive shape. Create a bark effect using a flower veining tool. Shape the green top into a ball and use the same texture mat that you used for the bushes to texture.

Anchor

Great for an underwater theme. This one is made using a cutter, but if you don't have a cutter, make by hand using gum paste.

Picket fence

Roll out some gum paste and use a pizza cutter to cut ribbons of paste for the uprights. Cut each one the same length, then trim to the undulated shape once you have them all lined up. Cut the supporting struts slightly thinner and leave to dry. Use royal icing to attach.

Shells

Make your own shells following the instructions on page 198 or make them using a mold. Molds are widely available on the Internet.

Seaweed

The seaweed could be made from gum paste (for free-standing seaweed strands) or modeling paste (for a softer effect). Use an X-acto knife to cut out the shape, working freehand if you are confident; if not, draw a template to follow.

Fish

Make a shoal of fish for an underwater-themed cake. They are cut using a cutter which embosses at the same time. These cutters are invaluable for making a large number of similar-shaped props.

Sand/Animal feed

This can be used for a number of themes. Follow the instructions for the straw, but before you leave it to dry, use a pizza cutter to slice into very fine pieces, spread them out and leave to dry.

Grass

Long grass works on all sorts of cakes. Roll the paste out fairly thickly as you want it to be able to stand up when dry. Cut triangles of different lengths and score down the center of the triangles with a flower veining tool. Bend the top over on a few.

Seaweed 2

A seaweed variation that is made either from gum paste or modeling paste to create an underwater garden. Using different colors and shapes adds interest.

Seaweed 3

Again, add texture and experiment with the shape to create another seaweed variation.

Making Props

- Plan the props at the same time as the toppers so you have the whole cake planned out and don't waste time making things that are unnecessary.

- Don't overdo the props; less is more!

- Spend as much time making the props as neatly and carefully as you would the animals. If they are not made well, they will let the whole scene down.

- Props are there to set the scene, so be creative. For example, you may wish to do a savannah scene with browns and golds rather than greens.

Acorn

Perfect prop for the squirrel on page 98 or for a woodland theme. Shape the nut from green gum paste. Add a pinch on the top. Make the cup from brown modeling paste and texture with a texture mat. Secure both pieces together with edible glue.

Feed troughs

Perfect for a zoo or a farmyard theme. Roll out the paste and cut a rectangle for the base of the trough, using a pizza cutter. Lay the paste over a rolling pin to dry. Cut the ends and attach together with edible glue. Add in the feed.

Sacks

Cute sacks made by rolling a sausage, flattening slightly and pinching the corners. Texture with a flower veining tool.

index

credits

· ·

Author's acknowledgments
I would like to thank Victoria Lyle, Kate Kirby and all the staff at Quarto Publishing for their support and encouragement to complete this book. I have thoroughly enjoyed making this book, not only in the making of all the animals but working with such delightful people.

I would like to dedicate this book to David, for many hours of fending for himself after a long day so he didn't have to break me off from creating creatures!